76258

P9-DFJ-239

Also by Jack Richardson:

Plays
The Prodigal
Gallows Humor
Lorenzo
Xmas in Las Vegas

MEMOIR OF A GAMBLER

Jack Richardson

Simon and Schuster · New York

Portions of this book have appeared previously in *Commentary, Esquire, Harper's, The New York Review of Books,* and *Playboy.*

Copyright © 1979 by Jack Richardson
All rights reserved
including the right of reproduction
in whole or in part in any form
Published by Simon and Schuster
A Division of Gulf & Western Corporation
Simon & Schuster Building
Rockefeller Center
1230 Avenue of the Americas
New York, New York 10020

Designed by Irving Perkins
Manufactured in the United States of America

1 2 3 4 5 6 7 8 9 10

Library of Congress Cataloging in Publication Data

Richardson, Jack, date.
   Memoir of a gambler.

   I. Title.
PZ4.R523Mo [PS3535.I3275]   813'.5'4   79-9378

ISBN 0-671-22584-7

To Elaine

Every decision acquired by the
ritually correct forms is a
"judgment of God."

—JOHAN HUIZINGA
Homo Ludens

Chapter I

Boethius, Walter Raleigh, Wilde, Sade—names that were going through my mind of those who had turned a prison cell into a work chamber. I sat hunched in an at-stool position on a concrete bench and wondered how anyone, after finding himself caged away by the world, would wish to maintain a literary dialogue with it. I had been in my cell only a few hours, and though I was foggy from lack of sleep, I felt a deeper enervation oozing through me. My reason for being confined was petty and laughable, and involved no real criminal volition on my part. Still, the green walls, sour air, and steel bars were parts of a geography I had often imagined myself in, and, after a while, this setting began to seem comfortable and in concord with the rest of my life. For over a year I had grown less and less inclined to do anything that required a decisive effort. That I hadn't completely desisted from the ordinary business of my life, was only because old habits of ambition were reluctant to abandon me.

Still, what work I did was minimal, based on rough standards of survival, and the idea of taking a thing seriously, of
smoothing it down, of reaching its conclusion—this I found
to be, often literally, sickening. What was left of the moral
advisor in me said I was letting things slide; his literary
counterpart mumbled about malaise and existential disquiet.
It was with the former I agreed; I *was* letting myself drift,
but not out of metaphysical fear and certainly not because
of esthetic principles. I am too intelligent to let a sensitive
thought process keep me from enjoying worldly pleasures.
No, it was not the universe that was failing me, I was failing it. In my scramble through indulgence, I was leaving behind me the usual refuse of the community of which I'm a
part: a divorce, a half-dozen or so squalid affairs, some literary jottings, one or two dedicated enemies, and the sense
of possibility that had got me started in the first place. Day
after day I mined myself and came up with nothing precious. Wanting to have my life weighed, analyzed, and pronounced rare, I had, by that famous nodal year of thirty,
found nothing conclusive about its samplings.

So slowly then I had let a deep fatigue take hold of me,
not just because I was frustrated with what I had not been
able to do, but also because I hoped that indifference might
bestir my personal fates. They may have been taking me for
granted as one who needed no providential signs, and I
wanted to demonstrate, with a little petulance, that I needed
as many as they could spare.

Well, in their usual way, they answered with no specifics,
but some hints had been dropped. While in semi-hibernation
one thing began to snap me into a state of keen sensitivity
over and over again. I had begun to gamble.

I am glad the last sentence is out of the way, for it is best
to get the subject of all this stated quickly and simply. While
my work, my friends, the leftovers of my family, my lady at

the time, the familiars of my apartment and neighborhood became dim and distant items, the sessions about a card or dice table, for as long as they lasted, created a clear, sensible landscape in which I felt solid ground under my feet. I don't mean to say that the landscape was hospitable. On the contrary, I tripped, stumbled, and left skin behind with almost each step. But the pain perked me up into bright consciousness, and for days afterwards I keenly examined the scabs left behind from my falls. At first I had taken the sessions at poker, dice, chemin de fer and blackjack played in private houses and well-locked back rooms around New York to be superficial diversions that kept me from mulling over the loose ends of the real life we are all supposed to have. Gradually, however, I saw they had a good chance of replacing it, for in a time of torpor, these moments at the table were providing me with the only hard evidence that I was indeed living.

I began slowly edging a new personality into the world. My clothes became tasteful, tailored and jaunty; my friends were treated to stories, some true, of high-rolling epics instead of indictments of contemporary literature. It was mostly comic acting, and I knew it at the time. But I also knew it was something more.

Gambling did not suddenly spring full-bloom into my life. When I was ten or eleven, my mother, who considered me extraordinary, gave me a miniature roulette wheel as a Christmas present. The table consisted of a small strip of cheesecloth with all the proper brackets and numbers painted on it. I've never known just why she picked out this particular toy; I don't remember asking for it. But as I said, she took me to be of a special cut and was always urging me to do outlandish things—such as learning Latin and tap dancing—to insure that I would never be mistaken for just another neighborhood boy.

The roulette wheel might have held my interest no longer than the month or so other toys received, had it not been for the pneumonia I caught some weeks afterwards. Confined to bed for two months, I took to spinning the small wheel for hours, marking down what numbers came up and trying to form infallible betting systems, an occupation excusable in a child. Also, the roulette wheel was a way of luring friends in for a visit. Ten-year-olds quickly tire of the bedridden, but when the convalescent provides a miniature casino they will put up with him. Most of my visitors were tiny Italian Catholics filled with senses of sin and evil, so they came eagerly to enjoy their little falls from grace. They put their pennies on the cheesecloth as though making offerings at a black mass, and I later had to pay for their sickroom company by being interdicted when I was on my feet again. One had confessed to his mother the squandering of six cents at the bedside of a Protestant gambler, and I thus became a sort of devil's agent to the Papists on Seventy-fourth Street in Jackson Heights.

The other gambling incident I recall from my childhood was more painful. One Saturday afternoon, behind a handball court at the local schoolyard, a group of older boys were having a craps game. After standing on its periphery for a time as befit my age, I drew up sufficient courage to inch forward close enough to watch the proceedings. As I looked down and saw at least five single-dollar bills waiting to be scooped up by the fortunate, I was overcome with greed of such intensity that I flew home, took my bicycle, and pedaled to a local shop where I sold it for ten dollars. Back to the schoolyard, again a moment at the edge of the onlookers, again dazzled by easy riches, and finally pushing beyond my proper station into the game. I knew nothing about dice except that seven was somehow a pivotal number, but my elders guided me honestly, despite being certain that such total innocence was bound to be rewarded. I disabused them of that theory in less than an hour. As wretched as I have ever been, I feigned a stoical retreat from the game, and then, once out of sight, cried in rage all the way home. It was too great a crime for me to live with alone, so still tearful, I threw myself on my mother's mercy. She was not angry, and in fact claimed to detect a trace of rare quality in the daring needed to gamble away a bicycle. The woman, as I said, wanted me to be extraordinary.

Though both these incidents form very sharp memories, neither I think slipped any real passion for gambling into my nervous system. If there was an early infection, then it was my grandfather who was the carrier. I saw him only once. My grandmother had given up on him and his profligate ways years before I was born. Tired of his week-long disappearances into card games that journeyed from Bristol, Virginia, to as far south as New Orleans, she finally came to New York, where several of our family had migrated, and went to work in a department store. When my mother was divorced in the same city, the three of us lived together until I was seventeen. Flanked and doted on by these two women, I was self-satisfied, spoiled, and happy; but I did at times yearn for a little masculine dash around the house. My father came to visit each week, but he did not really bring a heady male scent with him. He was a small man, cautious, a musician of indifferent talent who had once told me to "save myself for my wife," an admonition my mother would have disowned me for had I accepted it.

But my grandfather—there was a myth to be explored. A letter from him would set my mother and grandmother off on a whole evening's remembrance of his rapscallion ways. Though he had caused them both pain, I could see, even as a child, that they forgave and loved him. From what I gathered, he had lived a life of complete license, but he had once been shot in the stomach defending my grandmother from an enraged suitor disappointed that she had turned him down.

"With the bullet in him, he went right after that Jeffs boy, caught him in the street, and almost killed him."

Every time my grandmother said that line, she jerked her head emphatically at me and I knew I was receiving a code she expected me to live up to. I would nod solemnly, my mother would get that "be extraordinary!" look in her eyes, and then my grandmother would turn melancholy over the wandering card games. But soon the dirge would modulate into a light reminiscence about how that "devil" had put up his poultry farm in a stud game, lost it, and, before paying, had put together a chicken roast for the family and all its Negroes so that, as he said, he could cut down his losses with pleasure.

Well, here was a man as flawed as I knew I was and who still coaxed an abundance of love from the two women who watched over me. Perhaps then when all my weaknesses were exposed, perhaps when my mother realized that I was unlikely to be a published poet at the age of thirteen or the seducer of every maiden in the eighth grade, perhaps when my grandmother glimpsed that I, too, was very selfish, with wastrel ways and a disposition not to step in the line of fire between a woman and a madman—perhaps even then, if I could cultivate the roguish manner of grandfather, I'd still get my share of affection.

And then one day he came to visit. Miraculously tall, straight, with a hawklike countenance and a sea of white hair, he moved commandingly around our small apartment while both mother and grandmother scolded and giggled. I sensed a complete capitulation of morality to feeling, and that night he and my grandmother slept together. Though I was not certain what this meant, I felt a new well-being in the house.

During the stay, grandfather taught me the rudiments of stud poker while the ladies feebly protested. He was very grave about the instruction, for he was explaining a serious part of his life to a grandson. He had large, bony hands that made the cards dance about neatly on our little coffee table, and he spoke with soft conviction about how poker should be played, while every now and then, to propitiate my mother and grandmother, he threw in a caveat about the general dangers of gambling. The women feigned horror at the knowledge I was receiving, but I was certain they really felt pleased that should I ever be called into a poker game I could acquit myself like a gentleman—like a knowledgeable gentleman. As for grandfather, he had what he wanted—the center of the stage and a sense of importance. I found out later that nothing had been going too well for him down south—his friends were dying, his clubs were dropping him —so he had come north to verify that his life was still significant and perhaps even to enjoy a sense of family continuity through me. What skills he had to bequeath, he passed on in a few days, and, confident that I would never stay with a jack in the hole against a king and queen showing on board, he left his two ladies crying and returned to the existence he had fortified at our coffee table. In two years he died. The myth was complete. My grandmother had to pay for the funeral.

It was years before I put grandfather's advice to any practical use, and then I found it sadly inadequate. Also, in years of chatting with my grandmother much of the shine began to dim on the legend of Burt McDowell, Virginia Card Player. It was, I think, my first lesson in the stripping down of great men in order to expose human fears and needs.

19

Even now I am never anxious to uncover personal details about those men who taught me. The disappointment is too great, but not in the way Doctor Johnson meant when he chastised those who were shocked to find their favorite authors shabby in their private lives. He counseled that one should pay them double homage for overcoming the tainted nature of the species and achieving something superhuman in their work. No, I am not disappointed that the great ones are not sublimely excellent; but I am disheartened to find that, once known by me, they begin to pollute their own work. That a middle-aged pederast has fashioned a charming sestina out of a weekend with a sullen illiterate pulls the poem back into human folly and no amount of pure criticism is every going to restore it to a place of mysterious self-sufficiency.

Slowly, then, my grandfather and his gambling came down to human size. I saw a complicated poseur who used one frailty to hide another. It was better to be accused of social failure because of a propensity for the gambling tables than to have to admit that there were common things in the world you wanted but were too frightened or inept to attain. In the end he fervently desired to be buried in the Elks Club cemetery, hoping in death at last to be equal to those good, workaday citizens he felt so outmatched him in life.

Still, he had had enough slyness in his choice of disguises to leave two women with deep notions of love, and as I began to gamble, I looked back gratefully on him. His five-card stud instructions may have been faulty, but the other secrets he bequeathed me were more important. I knew that someday I, too, might really want my own piece of Elks Club cemetery rather than the wispy existence of one of luck's aging cavaliers. Even as I went off to a game in a glowing new suit, I took special effort to mock myself a little. All of this was only an interim to be enjoyed while the essential Jack Richardson revived himself and the real world again became a biting experience.

But there was no change. I rose each day, and without any fretting or self-recrimination, sat peacefully in my apartment for hours thinking about nothing more consequential than that indeed I was not fretful about the way time was being spent. What work I owed I postponed until it had to be churned out in a flush of rage over my being disturbed by it. I finally solved the problem of my days by sleeping through most of them, getting up at dusk, and gambling when I could until late in the morning. Gradually my reaction to the games I played in changed. Where before I had bet in a desultory manner, happy to be participating in something enjoyable, I now began to experience deep emotions over my fate in each outing. To lose filled me with such black feelings that only the sternest mental efforts could drag me back to the point where I would admit that a single loss had not turned me into one of gambling's lepers. And when I won, I felt as if a constellation in my image should appear in the morning sky. Also, I began taking a strange attitude toward money. Though I would carelessly toss it away in a game of poker, I began to keep meticulous records of where each bit of daily expense went. Each paper I bought, every tip I left, each call I made was marked down in an elaborate system of codes and categories. Then I would set off hoping that the night's action would let me come home and put down on paper that luck had picked up all my bills for the day. I would check and recheck these figures every afternoon, and I often worked well into the night, staring at the columns of numbers spread out on the floor, satisfied that I was imbibing vital information from them.

Soon my mind was in combat with itself, proposing arguments that gambling provides the answer to what all men want to know; namely, which of us are of the elect—and rebuffing this with cool reminders that since I'd never found any evidence for such a disclosure in the more traditional areas of life, it would be unlikely that something like divine determination would turn up in the theory of games. Occasionally during these debates, tired, old positivist arguments rose up on behalf of the semantic shakiness behind any absolute ranking of human behavior. I was not so far gone that such preoccupations with logical niceties did not make me feel a little foolish, but when I challenged this mental primness, I did so with little more than crude appeals to my own feelings, feelings which, at the time, I trusted very little.

And so with one part of my life beginning to fossilize, while the other blazed with a lunatic brightness, I arrived exhausted in a jail cell. I had been arrested in a raid on what the papers would later call a "fashionable Eastside gambling party." Those who had been caught with me were mostly young college boys who at first had enjoyed the notion of a trip to the station house and gayly exchanged jokes about crime and punishment. As we moved along in the police wagon, I had the slightly unclean feeling of the man who keeps company with those much younger than himself. I wondered if I might possibly look their coeval, thought back upon my life, and decided that it was unlikely.

At the station house my fellow companions' mood changed. When it became apparent that we really were to be booked and locked up until a hearing in the morning, they began to remember who they were or planned someday to be. Cries were imperiously made for lawyers and family intervention. But the authority they hoped for, when called, proved either too sleepy or too angry to take fast steps at intercession. Seeing that their move for power had failed, some of the young men fell to mournful questioning of the officers on how, since it was now Easter morning, they would get to Mass. This worked better, and though they still would have to be locked away for a while, assurances were given that they would be out in time to celebrate the resurrection of their Lord. I suppose they had hoped that a communion of faith would immediately free them, but calculating that their time in prison would be only hours, the band of fanatics went peacefully into their cells. And I, the reluctant agnostic, went calmly into mine.

I sat in the same delightful stupor that I did when forced to be alone and awake in my apartment. The notion that I was a bit absurd gnawed at me now and then, but my mind was too tired to be bothered by self-depreciating ironies. I would probably have dozed off like someone inured to frequent arrest had not the cell door opened and a new occupant arrived. I was startled into wakefulness. My companion was a beautiful black lady who glanced icily at me and, after a haughty heel-clicking walk, took the bench opposite mine.

Now I was not in a lustful mood but I was excited by the notion of my enjoying, right under the noses of a constabulary caught on their holy day, some infidel delights. There was not much time for courtship, so I got up and tried to shuffle pleasantly toward her. She fixed me with a mean eye that made me stand in place for a while. I wanted to tell her that she had made me move with a semblance of purpose for the first time, apart from a gambling room, in many months, but I suspected the compliment would take too long to explain.

"What are you in for?" I said, choking a little on the cliché. But there was no answer, only a sullen look. Back to the shuffle, and my fingers were soon lightly touching her shoulder. There was no attempt to remove them, so I began to fondle her arm until I came to the hand. It was suspiciously large and powerful. Slowly I began to wonder if it were customary for our moral police to put men and women into a cell together, even for a few hours.

I stood up.

"Are you a man?" I asked.

"You better believe it, baby," was the answer in a voice so *basso* that it propelled me back to my corner of the cell. My sense of manners kept me from laughing. Fooled by a transvestite! Here in a cell, worn out from years of trying to define with greater and greater precision all the high thoughts and feelings of the world—here I find I can be duped by a sullen drag queen in a ten-dollar dress.

Bertrand Russell once said that, during a walk in an English garden, he altered, in five minutes, his entire social philosophy. Nothing so drastic happened to me because of that Easter morning encounter. I am a bit slower, perhaps, than Lord Russell, so that it took a few weeks before I renounced catechizing over gambling and gave in to what I instinctively felt would bring me fully back to life.

Once my mind had been made up, it became full of pragmatic purposes. My plan was to start west, go first to Las Vegas and then on to California. After that, my itinerary would be decided by good or bad luck.

My mind then wanted immediate travel, but I first made it put old skills to work and calculate percentages and methods of play at each game I would be likely to encounter. I wasn't going to be one of Fortuna's corybants. I wanted to present her with well-reasoned wagers that showed I took nothing, least of all her good mathematical sense, for granted.

At other times, of course, I envisioned a single blind play, one all-or-nothing wager. I would dress slowly and impeccably, as though preparing for a formal ritual. Then, after caressing and counting the money, I would place it neatly in my pocket and walk, with the economy of purpose of an assassin, to the table grand enough to accept my bet. After selecting what I wished to play, I would lay the money lightly down, gaze only briefly at its resting place in limbo between me and the bank, and then lift my eyes upward, disdaining concern over the man-made apparatuses that would punish or reward me, knowing that judgment would not come from them. At this point, when the wheel began to spin or the cards snap toward me, things became too vivid to be endured even in imagination. I would force these dangerous images from my mind and hurry back to the security of my equations.

And then, every few days or so, I would wonder if I might very well be going insane, especially when, at night, old voices asked for a justification.

"I want to know," I would answer them. "I want finally to know."

They would then scratch out: "What do you want so badly to know?"

And I would answer: "Whether I am to have any grace in this life."

At this, the voices changed into rueful sighs and expired into silence.

The voices could never persuade, but they could depress me. They made me dwell on what I had decided to leave behind with only a faint chance that my future life would ever allow a reclamation. My daughter—lanky, nervous and beautiful, before whose gaze there was no protest articulate enough for my exoneration; my ex-wife, wise and stubborn, who had not used the grim knowledge our marriage had given her to hurt me; the girl who loved me now, who sensed that it would end soon, but made no scene—they had all come into my life at times when I had faltered in my self-absorption. Now they would recede along with all that I could not bring to the tables with me.

The last night, while she slept, I lay awake. There is nothing so still as a room one is about to leave perhaps forever. The quiet is spread out and heavy as though offering a foretaste of what will be left behind when the waves floating from the click of the outside latch exhaust themselves against the walls. I think I was as calm that night as I had ever been in my life. The body next to me was warm and curved to fit snugly against mine; through the bedroom door I could see my books stacked in the library and the furniture that had come to stay bit by bit over the past years. On my desk, there was a folder that I had abandoned for months. In it were some sketches for a project that I had forgotten to store with all those literary schemes I no longer wished to attempt. The girl moaned and stretched next to me. I looked down and smiled at her. Work on the table; a loved girl in bed; and rooms fashioned into a sanctuary. It was an old voice warming to a last try.

I didn't bore the quietness with fancies about grace or fortune; I admitted that all the chaos I was going into frightened me and that I might someday grow numb even to the pleasures of gambling. I was heading west in the morning simply to prove that the peace surrounding me was not my final fate.

Chapter II

During the summer of my tenth year, my father fastened on LaGuardia Airport for our Sunday outings. We would walk from my neighborhood across the vast empty lots of wartime Queens until we reached the air terminal's observation platform, and there, like two otiose pensionnaires, we would sit out the hot afternoons watching planes land and depart. My father, being a musician, had traveled the routes of small jazz bands in his youth, and this had forever soured him on wandering, so that it was not from any desire to cross horizons that he coaxed me to the airport on visiting days: he simply loved the machines and the mystery of aerodynamics. Although in later life he was to become a religious fundamentalist, certain he could feel in every finger the soul God gave him, he was at that time a worshiper of all the two- and four-engined totems in the air, and he could sit for hours, windblown and baked, in aboriginal awe of the great metal birds. Though at the time I had no idea why, this weekly excursion caused a strange uneasiness in me. While my father looked upward in wonder, I was fretfully glancing around us, observing movement, watching people weighted down by no more than the luggage they carried vanish into the sky and head for the world's secrets which I was even then frightened I might never discover. I felt I certainly wouldn't if these Sunday afternoons were any indication of my future. Everything around us was in exciting flux, while we sat in what seemed to me pedestrian and shameful stasis, and I squirmed uncomfortably in the heat while trying to reassure myself that I, too, would be one day set into motion. It is a painful moment when a child comprehends through his parents that life need not end in heroic action, and in the nightmares I remember having that summer, dying was no longer synonymous with dizzying falls into darkness, but rather with any object completely at rest. A stone set heavily in an empty field, a chair solidly occupying the center of a room, my apartment building—a paralysis of Spanish Colonial style—these were now the images of mortality that haunted my sleep.

The mark that those Sundays laid upon me became an important feature of my life. I could not, for example, accept an academic existence when it was offered me, because to remain at the still point of a professorship while cycles of students passed by would have been a contradiction of my notion of existence as a distance to be traveled and explored. Evidence that I am living comes to me only by turning with the planet I am on, and I have always looked forward to a life of flight while the dumbstruck and grounded like my father vanished behind me. Rilke has said ". . . *so leben wir und nehmen immer Abschied*"—so we live, always taking leave. The poet was saddened by this, but then his memory possessed a rare vitality and all he took leave from stayed with him, painful in being near and irretrievable. I do not like to think that I am of coarser stuff than Rilke, but my leave-takings almost render me an amnesiac; all before my departure slips into neutralizing shadow while I look ahead to the mysteries of a new geography. One knows, of course, that the past will make its claim, but if we are not poets, these hauntings will be vague, producing a melancholy soothed by prose rather than an anguish that demands poetry.

All this is to say that I was very happy the day I left for Las Vegas. Moving out on the Long Island Expressway, I looked back toward New York and could see all my past tucked away among the tall buildings. The dialectic was now over; I was a gambler heading for a sympathetic environment, and all the Byzantine puzzles as to what had set me off were put aside as Kennedy Airport appeared and I thought how it was only on these great flat spreads of land, where things in transit meet the least friction, that modern architecture is truly beautiful.

After I had checked my lone suitcase, I strolled, without even the encumbrance of a magazine, through the terminal. I felt the nonchalance of the tyrant who reeks invincibility to the point that he can walk among his slaves unarmed. I had the whole world in which to follow my fortune, and I needed no heavy ordnance for the chase. However, I had in my inside coat pocket a small stash of necessary supplies: a notebook that would be used to mark down the balance of victory and defeat each day, and my wallet, containing $15,280 in First National City Bank traveler's checks, and $2,200 in cash. Earlier that morning, while stuffing it with this treasure, I had discovered, in one of my wallet's hidden compartments, a silver dollar. Since it had been years since I'd carried silver in anything but my pockets, I had no idea where the coin came from. For a moment I'd thought of keeping it for luck, but then, considering the coin too commonplace to earn me any favors, I had reduced my stake by one unit and left it behind, proud that not one gambler in a thousand would have had the will to turn his back on such an inviting amulet. But I wanted at the time to have nothing to do with charms and fetishes. I had descended to the plane of practical strategy. As I have said, I did not want to be a mystic at the tables, dropping chips at random as though the heavens owed me happy endings. However, I was also loath to become the victim of some involved mathematical system that tries, through binomial camouflage, to squirm around the fact that almost every bet in a casino carries odds against it. What I had charted for myself was a loose decalogue for gambling in Las Vegas. It was written down in my notebook as follows:

(1.) You shall not play roulette, for the odds of the wheel are prohibitive.

(2.) You shall not, under pain of self-loathing, go past a thousand dollars in losses on a given night.

(3.) You shall allow wagers to run high enough so that courage is shown and felt, but not so high that retribution can be excused by an excessive folly.

(4.) You shall be clearheaded in the temple, even if free drinks are proffered and your nerves are of a jangle.

(5.) You shall, at the craps table, bet only those chances which come closest to being of an even nature. Cast out those bets of *Field, Hardway Fours, Any Craps, Big Six* and *Big Eight*, for they are the true demons, especially when you are behind.

(6.) You shall not be at the tables more than five consecutive hours. Zeal is expected of you, but the fanatic is coolly received in heaven.

(7.) You shall dress carefully for the casinos and not loosen your tie after a heavy loss. In control there is confidence, and from that comes courage.

(8.) You are allowed, within limitations, carnal pleasures, but only after you have finished the day's playing. Successful coitus has always tended to make you smug and careless.

(9.) You shall not feel obliged to abstain from silent prayers and curses, for it is by these that the gods know a man is serious in his petition of them.

(10.) You shall, finally, remember these to have been written when the mind was tranquil and confident. If they are broken by you under strain of loss or exultation, remember that the scriptures for your life are flexible.

I was pleased looking over these precepts. Though they had been contrived out of no more urgency than a need to pass time, they seemed civilized enough to meet the spiritual complexities of a casino. However, when a voice called out my flight number, and I suddenly knew it was all to begin, I hurriedly wrote, in small letters beneath them, the word "please." I laughed at my doing this as I boarded the plane, but I felt relieved that I had been able, without affectation, to ask for kind treatment and a traveler's blessing.

Once before I had come to Las Vegas, and had been, in two senses, overwhelmed; first, by the town itself, then by the blackjack tables. I had arrived to do a show-business-personality story for a magazine, but that mission quickly faded into secondary importance as soon as I stepped into the casino of one of the hotels. The only other time that I had been in a public room devoted to gambling had been in Nice's Municipal Casino, and that event, occurring while I was a student on summer holiday, had almost fatally wounded the entire European trip by costing me eight hundred dollars. But the environment for that misfortune had been hushed, self-contained, almost indifferent to the presence of innocents who are certain that a few hours of roulette will allow them to stay at first-class hotels for the rest of their summer tour. Quite different were the Las Vegas casinos; they belched out greetings like a local politician. There were long howls at the dice tables, the whir and jingle of the slot machines, the music from the lounge and, as a droning bass counterpoint, the dealers' voices cajoling bets and announcing wins and losses. In a matter of hours I was drugged into being an obedient tourist and lost three times what I was to be paid for probing the soul of the celebrity my magazine was interested in.

Now, on the plane, heading for a second joust with Las Vegas, I thought back on that time, and spread balsam over the memory by recalling that this first defeat had occurred at precisely the time when my entire life was in general rout. To begin with, I had just experienced a near unextenuated public failure as a playwright, and since I do not, where it concerns writing, have a great deal of inner mail or visionary passion to sheathe me from concern over even intimated criticism, the frontal volley I received when I staged a dramatic comedy about art and war had made me want to closet every thought away before it could be turned into prose, discovered, and ridiculed. And, too, the collapse of the play was of double weight, for it came at a time when I was beginning to sniff out some of the pleasures of success. For five years, in the manner of the dedicated German novelist, I had lived in the constricted world of work and family. My wife had given me the self-obliterating devotion that could be justified only by my being the author of a new *Iliad*, and I sat in the middle of our small world in alternating terror and disdain of the larger one. Gradually, however, as what I wrote allowed me to swagger a bit under the promising-young-writer label, I began scurrying about New York, a minor piece of promise upending as many ladies as he could impress, and, out of shallow exuberance, professing love to them all—a habit that soon set my telephone at home ablaze with lamentations and cryptic messages which my wife often received. There was no need, however, for her to decipher the various codes of insult and disappointment, for I was feckless enough to deny nothing, and indeed pumped up my transgressions like an old lady in fantasy. In sulky remorse I would come home each morning, rouse her from sleep, evacuate the night's intrigue, ask for the understanding I was sure her college education had given her, promise to enter psychoanalysis, and then doze off swollen with innocence.

Still, if I could use the hearth as a refuge from conquest, I was not so low as to turn it into a retreat once again from a predatory world. With my promise beginning to peel, I couldn't go back into lonely *Kulturkampf* with, as my only ally, a woman whom I had brutalized with inexpensive truths. Searching for some moral sanction, I came up with the desire to bear this difficult time alone so that whatever excesses I committed would hound only myself. Thus, taking half of our furniture, I separated from my wife and, stunned that I had actually done something so decisive, moved into a small, bleak apartment on the Westside of New York, thinking that there, in solitude, I could reassemble myself.

It was not a success. As for my work—well, I always had had difficulty overcoming the notion that I was a charlatan as an artist. I had no special way of seeing the world—indeed, I distrusted unique perspectives because they argued a mind with a poor imagination for alternatives. Whenever I set forth to cast a tale about the dilemma of being, it would occur to me that perhaps we are all really meant for a heaven where we shall be forever twenty-one, perfectly featured, and blessed by the knowledge that everything has worked out as the celestial nous intended. Hoping for grotesque and vigorous insights in my Westside apartment, I discovered that I was still a classic rationalist, a person

33

suited to the conditional rather than the emphatic style. Somehow, the true writer must consider his art absolutely important, must believe that the search for appositeness, for the balance of a made-up world, for the rhythm and drama of punctuation is serving something more than itself. One can talk about style and "esthetic bliss," but there can be no bliss without some prior cognition, for only a deranged mind will not demand some meaning before it dissolves into ecstasy. Thus, no matter how he connives, the writer must feel that he has something to remark upon living and dying that is significant enough to justify all the fuss of language. This belief in significance has, I admit, produced some of the worst art among our canon of classics, but without it I don't see how there could be any art at all.

I, unfortunately, lacked that belief totally. I could simulate it for the duration of a work perhaps, but I knew that it was not real, that everything I conjured was by calculation, and that I meant not a word of it. Finally, every sentence I wrote winked back at me from the page like a coy conspirator, and I stopped altogether, ready, like Valéry, for a twenty-year hiatus of honest silence.

Meanwhile, I was attending to myself. I had entered psychoanalysis where I was finding out such facts as that my fear of the sound of birds' wings could be traced to the rustle of my mother's dress and that the inordinate time I was then spending in poolrooms was a homosexual indicator. To offset this last discovery and to propitiate the ghost of my mother, I was furiously conducting affairs with two women who shared my recently separated category. The older of the pair enjoyed acts of outright lunacy. I remember the months with her to be filled with continual claims of pregnancy, punches, wounds, sutures, weepings and all types of hysteria on both our parts. At first when she would rise off into rage,

34

I would counter by pretending to be madder than she was. It somehow calmed her when I dropped to my knees after she'd successfully hurled some object at my head and began a convulsive account of how I had been tortured in an Army prison. I would talk wildly and sob for an hour while she, calmed by my simulated breakdown, issued good, sensible commands to get hold of myself. Gradually, however, I found I had to spend more and more time pretending to greater and greater derangement. I became insecure about managing the transitions, and so said goodbye to the lady. Again there was an accusation of impregnator, and, as I fled down the stairs from her apartment, a lethally full garbage pail missed my temple by inches.

The younger woman, whom I called Lady Bountiful, made it clear that she wanted to be raped of all self-esteem. Falling back on the *acte gratuit* philosophy of my student days, I played the cold gigolo with her. I could not believe I had actually found another human being in worse condition than I was at the time, but Lady B proved me wrong. No matter how much money I took from her or how many times she was abandoned after dinner or at a party while I went off with someone else, she would always rush back into the strappado the next day. She was dark, not particularly pretty, with a propensity to bathe less frequently than she should, but she was bright—bright enough to realize that for all she gave, there was not even a real person there with his hand out to snap it up. She liked to say she was a gambler, and indeed I remember forcing her to play for high stakes at chemin de fer while I blatantly cheated. She, however, refused to notice, marveled at my luck, and when I set off the first time for Las Vegas, she gave me two thousand dollars to play with and took me to Dunhill's to be outfitted in linen jackets in order that I might glow in racy elegance while winning a fortune. Happily, while I was gone, she went back to her husband and never asked after the money or the suits.

Thus the coloring around my first trip to Las Vegas. A sad benefactress, a broken marriage, a one-woman psychodrama, a self-excluding theory of art, a basement apartment —one hundred dollars a month, including a rug, air-conditioner and access to a cement yard where one could sunbathe among bottles and other neighborly debris—among these calamities the loss at the blackjack tables seemed no ill omen. I was in general decline, and, like the financial market, sound stocks as well as bogus ones went down with me.

But the decline was over. I was now on my way, and I believed all accounts with the past had been fairly settled. The pilot announced that the Mississippi River was beneath us, and I was filled with Midwestern exuberance. I would soon be meeting Las Vegas again, and the only resemblance between me and the man they had humbled three years before would be the Lady Bountiful jackets from Dunhill's.

I arrived at close to five in the afternoon. As we circled to land, I looked down on the small clump of buildings surrounded by nothing, and felt just a twitch of fear. One can hardly believe in the appearance of a Las Vegas in such wilderness. There's no natural reason—no river, no lake, no snug valley—to justify its existence in all that space. And then suddenly you realize that you are its reason for being, you are the effective cause of its irrigated golf courses, its billion volts of neon, its ganglia of hotels, its bands, comedians, shills, hookers and instant marriage chapels, of all that complicated circus which beckons you into the desert. I looked from my plane window and for a moment felt that the first dragon sent forth to test the quester's resolution was too much for him. The money that had been a sword in Kennedy Airport seemed now feeble weaponry against the city beneath me, and it was only after reminding myself of my commandments, and of the fact that I was not here to do battle but to be blessed, that my ebullience returned. After all, I was not laying siege, but adroitly courting favor.

On the way to my hotel, however, as we passed great explosions of colored concrete—hotels in which one knew millions of dollars waited for the one who could confound the laws of probability—the Icarus in every gambler was beginning to slip on his wings. But I clipped them quickly, pulled myself away from the million-dollar sun, and decided there, in the taxi, that I would try for no more than ten thousand dollars here in Nevada, and would give myself, say, four days to do it in. Then, if the worst happened and I lost my thousand-dollar maximum every night, I stood only to lose four thousand dollars as against making a potential ten. Of course, I knew that I was projecting rough estimates, but some boundaries had to be set lest I doom myself to an infinity of play and inevitable death from the house vigorish.

There were two other passengers in the cab, both boys of about nineteen who had met on a flight from Los Angeles. One was thin, with a hungry, youthful face beneath a greased pompadour several inches high. He was wearing a clean T-shirt, boots, jeans, and Marine tattoos on each arm. He had a Southwestern drawl and when he spoke, which wasn't often, his voice showed he was embarrassed at being in an informal situation with those who must have seemed like extensions of the Marine officers he'd saluted and sirred month after month. I pictured him, his Marine cap at a tilt, very drunk on beer, buying "tea" for some whore twenty years his senior who might or might not have compassion enough to give him the five-minute screw needed to send him back to his base with a feeling of accomplishment. He had come from Los Angeles to Vegas, as he put it, "Just to do some lookin'," but his nonchalance was no more genuine than mine. The tattoos, the hair, the little swirls of booze lines under the young eyes—I had known so many like him when I was in the Army. They had somehow always met with official disaster—courts-martial, restrictions to base for the remainder of their tour because of excessive encounters with gonorrhea, or put out in an infantry platoon to be killed.

His companion was his antithesis. Tall, firmly built, blond, with a profusion of freckles to distinguish his skin rather than primitive markings, he spoke in a pure, clean California accent on how he was here to work on a dude ranch during school vacation and how it was impossible to win money in Las Vegas.

"Oh, you can have fun losing," he said cheerfully, "if you don't go too far, I mean. If you want to drop ten or twenty dollars—and you will!—go ahead. Anything more than that is just stupid."

The ex-Marine smiled like one who knew he would wake up in his motel, hung-over, broke, forced to set out to find a job in one of the used-car lots or Western Union offices. All his life there had probably been some educated, reasonable voice giving him good counsel, and he had probably always smiled to hide the shame he felt in knowing that he could not follow it.

"Don't try to win any money now. Just go see the shows," said the boy on vacation as the Southerner got out at a small motel.

"I'll just do some lookin' first," said the other. "And I'll see them shows."

Two young men—one indifferent to annihilation, the other, for all his optimistic freckles, already calculating how best to minimize inevitable losses. I stood between them with my ten-thousand-dollar limit, not certain which was the better brother in arms.

When I entered my hotel, I pointedly kept my eyes away from the casino. This was my first, small exercise in discipline, and its success pleased me. The opening wager of the journey wasn't going to be tossed compulsively away. Some small bit of form had to attend it, and I wanted at least to be unrumpled and clean for the ceremony.

I got to my room, unpacked carefully, then undressed and spread myself out on the cool, silk coverlet of the bed whose size was great enough for easy *à trois* accommodations. It was lovely lying there, a cupped hand protecting my crotch from the air conditioning, savoring these last unbloodied moments before, at my choosing, it would all begin with an inconspicuous twenty-dollar bet at the dice table. It is sad, I thought, that one can't remain always in anticipation, always ready for a great action, and always free to will exactly when that action shall begin. If Cyrus, Xerxes, or the others who enjoyed the high old ancient powers had a special blessing, it was simply that they could be poised at all times to shatter an empire, to know the deed was just a breath in front of them, and, knowing this, could fall back, certain of history, into a large, comfortable bed.

For the first time, I think, I felt a despot over my own life, and, to celebrate, I almost called the bellboy to accept his offer to provide me company when wanted. But then I remembered my eighth commandment and the desire for imperial amusement melted in my hand. I got up, showered, dressed with military abruptness, placed the checks and cash in my pocket, and, with sober thoughts, headed for the casino.

My hotel, like most in Las Vegas, had grown by lateral additions, so that there are interminable corridors to walk before one arrives at the casino focal point. It was now nearly seven o'clock. The sun, which I looked at through the glass wall, was beginning to ease downward toward the flat land. The swimming pool was empty and darkened by shadows. The neon was on, mixing well with the Western dusk. Those who used the days of Las Vegas were being flushed back toward the hotel by coming darkness: golfers, tennis players, bathing-suited mothers with exhausted children—the sun-tanned people of life.

But I didn't begrudge them their health, their fresh melanic pigment, their money or their laughter. At the tables we would all be equal, and a pale, stooped intellectual stood as much a chance for favor as the most robust, golden athlete.

Suddenly, a turn in the corridor, and the casino was in front of me. The same noises, the same tangle of players, tables and wheels that I had remembered. Now, however, the room didn't overpower me. I had come with it in mind, had seen it every night in my imagination for the past week. I was not being cajoled into the pit; I was climbing in by choice.

I went to the cashier's cage and put the traveler's checks in a safety-deposit box. If all went well, I thought, I would never have to use them. I moved on and stood for a time next to a blackjack table where a group of ladies giggled and moaned every time the dealer outdrew them. The dealers! As I walked along the tables I looked at them—the blank, indifferent angels handing out judgments with each card, with each spin, with each roll. I knew now that most of them once had been players against the house and had been broken. So, to live for a time, they had stepped to the safe side of the table and never came back. I looked at their professional costumes and tried not to imagine myself similarly outfitted by defeat.

I went on past two large roulette tables, hardly ever in

play, since even the most untutored gamblers in Las Vegas have heard that the American wheels have two numbers that win for the house while those in Europe have only one. Not that percentages mean that much to most vacation players who will cheerfully take worse odds on certain bets at the craps table. It is rather that here the swindle is easily recognized by all, and only a few old ladies addicted to the game were indifferent enough to being considered simple-minded to challenge the strength of zero and double zero.

And then I was at a craps table which only five players were using. It might as well all begin here, I thought, and without taking my wallet from my coat I extracted a hundred-dollar bill and folded it carefully in my hand. I didn't want one of the croupiers to catch a glimpse of it and bellow an offer of change. I wished to make the announcement that I was there to gamble precisely when I felt the urge to do so. I was not inflating this act with deep portent, but neither did I want to be bustled into my first bet. I watched the dice pass hands until they came to a young girl who was playing with her husband. They were betting two dollars at a time and not really understanding when they won or lost. Since the pace was slow at the table, one of the stickmen undertook to advise the girl, after she'd made a successful pass, about the benefits of "Behind-the-Line" bets—a wager that receives its proper odds. When she won again he shifted his instruction to the *Come Line* and how one can go from there to secondary bets on the numbers. Her husband smiled warily as the betting became more complex and his chips were scattered around the table on squares that seemed far away from the simplicity of one win or one loss. However, his wife made two more passes and was being schooled on odds when I handed the bill to another croupier and asked for a stack of twenty-dollar chips.

It was almost time to begin. The girl made another pass

41

and squealed delightedly while her husband frowned at seeing part of the winnings go back into another bet. Getting ready for her next roll, she clacked the dice furiously, and before they flew out from her hand, I had put twenty dollars behind the *Don't Pass Line*. I was betting against her, and the croupier, as part of his lesson, pointed this out, which caused her to give me an injured look. I glanced away, not wanting to share this moment with any particular person. I would have preferred the casino empty, with the dice moving by themselves at random across the table.

Not realizing the size of the event she was part of, the girl did not vanish, but instead bounced the dice down the table. They came up four, a point that now made me a two-to-one favorite. On her next three rolls neither a four nor a crap-out seven appeared. On and on she tossed, making every point but those affecting us, until I felt that there was no longer anything extraordinarily special about the twenty dollars I had placed on the green felt. I watched the dice like any other player with something at stake on them, thinking about nothing but the sight of a winning seven, and what was left of the ceremonial beginning was washed away as the girl finally rolled a deciding number.

It was a four. I had lost.

A craps table is like a medieval chart of the elements, an involved design that contains all the categories of chance a pair of dice can create. It is covered with squares within squares, numbers within boxes and circles, and phrases in hermetic jargon that describe the nature of the bet each area of the table accommodates. Compared to the classical order of the roulette table whose thirty-six variables are neatly arranged, colored and classified, and where, like the square root of two or some other Pythagorean embarrassment, zero and its ambiguity are banished outside the main order of things—compared to this symmetry, that of the craps table is a Gothic clutter of symbol, sign and word, a product of many anonymous architects who founded their structure on the caprices and whims of generations of gamblers. The table that evolved attracts a rowdy following, always standing, jostling and howling while they look for the right place in the maze before them on which to place their money. A Voltaire might have enjoyed the wistful dreams of roulette and the comic calculations of its players, but he would have been put off by the sweat and superstition of the crapshooter caught in a patchwork of deceptive symbols.

And now the raucous crapshooter had found a leader. The girl I was betting against had made a fourth pass, and her squeals and the applause of those who rode her luck at the table knelled an invitation through the casino which more and more players accepted. The aisles filled with those looking for something better than their own fortune to follow and they either mirrored what the girl did or else found some combination in sympathy with her intuitions. Men mostly, in shirtsleeves and string ties, and a few tough, tanned, bejeweled casino termagants, fastened themselves to the table and sent their money scuttling across the board while encouraging the girl on to further victories. The croupier, who a few minutes before had been giving her counsel, now watched coldly, apprehensive that he might have been a tutor to a catastrophe.

I was the only person still betting against the shooter, and when I put my fifth twenty-dollar chip down on the *Don't Pass Line*, I was met all about with dark stares, as though I were cursing the community's good fortune. Already eighty dollars behind, I could stand defeat at the table but not hostility. I thought for a moment of switching my bet so that it conformed to the general persuasion, but that desire to be unique, which had caused me so much pain in the past, swelled up to keep me and my twenty dollars in noble minority.

This roll I won and I left the table. I felt deflated. I had naturally hoped that my first turn would be a winning one, but the sixty-dollar deficit I now marked in my mind was only a minor barb. More disconcerting was the vapid frivolity of the girl and the low-bred frenzy of those who had backed her. I had anticipated my initiation for so long, and now I felt it had been robbed of its dignity. I stood in the middle of the casino and its rude noises, and felt outraged that I and my money might dissolve away in such a room, leaving no trace, no mark behind that would be memorable. In the last year I had always been able to remove the sting from such moments by taking a cold, mocking, objective look at myself. However, this time I indulged in dramatics. I left the casino and took my fear of oblivion out into the desert night, past the swimming pool and onto the first tee of the golf course. There I wallowed peacefully in sad mortal thought.

"That is God," my mother had said to me, pointing to the same sky some twenty years ago. We were in Arizona on one of our many trips to look for a new home in a sunny climate. "All of that up there is God."

I remember her saying this, and I suppose it was in response to a question of mine, for my mother rarely indulged in such speculations, preferring to definite religious teachings a fine shade of pantheism that placed divinity in the stars but excused it from abiding in mud, rocks and other ignoble matter. Probably, foggy from the day's motor trip, upset over being dislocated, and constipated from having sat for hours in the back of our Plymouth, I had not been able to sleep in the motel bed, and, anxious for company, had roused my mother with what I knew to be a question too serious to be put off or rebuked for. If this was so, I paid dearly for the ruse: my mother might have taken comfort in a god coextensive with a night sky, but this image disconcerted me. I was looking for a much more palpable presence. For months, without telling anyone, I had begun wondering about God, but there had been certainly no visions of unending galaxies in my mind. Like Pascal, the dark spaces terrified me, and I was happy when we left the West and returned home to New York where the buildings, soot and fog choked the sense of divinity from the sky.

However, for months afterward, my mother's definition continued to upset me. I had never before questioned her rightness about the things of the world I needed to learn, but this time, knowing that there was at least an alternative to what she had told me, I went on with my own investigations. Cautiously, as it was a delicate point between us, I began questioning my Catholic friends on what their notions of God were, but where their church had always had a healthy appetite for converts, these young Italians met my curiosity with laconic suspicion.

"Jesus Christ is God," was all I ever got as an answer, and this small concession was generally offered with a look that clearly told me that I, who sat in no catechism class, attended no Mass, made no confessions, and was thus marked for the Hell they already knew so vividly, I was putting them in great jeopardy merely by coaxing them to utter the name of their Lord in my presence. Now, I certainly knew who Christ was, having sung about Him every Christmas at school, and my mother, while shearing Him of divinity, had often paraphrased for me the official chronicles of His life and allowed that He was a very good man. Still, it took months of inquiry and baffling reading before I felt that

45

He might be the companion, and His church the sanctuary, I was looking for.

As I said, conversion was not easy. I knew that there was a proper procedure involved, but since those privy to its secrets were not disposed to share them with me, I floundered for months in alternating terror of celestial infinity and the graphic inferno in which I would end were I not to wheedle my way somehow into the sanctity of the True Church. And then, finally, I found my missionary. His name was Gino, a boy a year older than myself who enjoyed the worst of reputations in our neighborhood. He was a known thief, an insolent student, a dirty fighter and the deflowerer of a thin, ugly, retarded girl named Betty, whom he allowed others, on payments ranging from a dime to a quarter, depending on her position, to look at naked. With all these honors on, Gino found it difficult to have friends. Ours was not a neighborhood of hard poverty and violence, and though the manly virtues of the streets were preached in theory by my friends, they hoped, in secret, for respectable futures. Gino looked definitely headed for reform school, and this was enough to frighten us all away from him. Apparently, however, he did not enjoy the solitude of the strong, and, every few months or so, he fastened onto someone whom he made into a reluctant associate and confidant.

"Hey, meet me tonight and we'll see what's doing on Roosevelt Avenue," he would say, and since a refusal meant both blood and the definite admission that Gino's life was too dangerous for one, he always got his temporary companion. The enjoined comradeship would last for about a month, after which Gino either tired of such a concentrated relationship or perhaps felt sorry for the one pressed into service. As capriciously as he had been chosen, the boy was discarded and another took his place.

I knew my time had come when Gino walked up to me after school one Friday and offered to let me witness the mysteries of Betty for nothing. As had all the others, I obeyed the command, and that evening, after lying to my mother about a school party, I met Gino in front of an apartment building and followed him down into the basement where Betty, sniffing asthmatically in the cellar dust, was waiting in a storage bin. Since, except for quick glimpses of my mother, I had never seen a naked female body before, I was quite excited, and the knowledge that Gino was buying me with this spectacle was a small price to pay for such experience.

Placing her clothes in a baby carriage, Betty began to undress as soon as we arrived. She had a long, pale, acned face that I had always seen wearing glasses. For the occasion, however, she had removed them and I noticed that her eyes were by no means exactly synchronized. There was no question of her ugliness, but an eleven-year-old in search of sexual experience is not too fastidious. I was even set tingling when, after removing her dress, she stood in nothing save undershirt and sagging pink bloomers, both of which were torn and not very clean.

"You want everything off, Gino?" she asked.

"Sure, Jack's a friend of mine. Everything off."

Yes, yes—I was indeed a friend of Gino's!

In the next instant she was naked. No man who knows he's sold his soul for the ashes of earthly pleasures ever felt more horror than I did as those ragged undergarments fell away and Betty presented me with my first look at the swells and declivities of a woman. She stood, slouched and sullen, exposing an emerging pubescent body dotted with moles. She was breastless, and when, with numb compulsion, I glanced down at what I had heard so much magic whispering about, I

47

found hardly a hairy diadem, but rather a sparsely tufted mound which made me think of two thick eyebrows raised in sudden shock.

"Do you want me to take different positions?" she said, starting to pirouette her thin body.

"You can feel her up if you want," Gino said, beaming with friendship. I remember how my head was spinning, how sick I felt, and I'm amazed that I kept my manly composure. I said something to the effect that I had already felt up a girl, knew what it was like and all, and didn't want to abuse my friend's generosity. This pleased Gino and he offered to let me watch while he did advanced things to Betty there in the storage bin. Now, I have not yet said that another reason for Gino's lack of natural popularity was the fact that he was thyroidally fat, weighing nearly two hundred pounds at the age of twelve, and the thought of that amplitude coupled in some mysterious way with Betty sent me, panicked by sensuality, running out of the basement.

Outside, in the fresh air, some reason returned. I didn't want it bruited about that I was scared by the shadows over Eden. And further it seemed politic not to vanish completely, for Gino was as unpredictable at taking offense as he was at making friends. Shivering with sweat, I waited, trying to get back some of the nonchalance stripped from me by Betty's *mons Veneris*.

In a few minutes Gino appeared and ordered me to follow him. He was walking quickly, and I thought his pace connoted anger with me for having rudely left the party he'd prepared. I started to apologize, but he didn't seem interested. He was in a deep brood, and for some reason I could tell it wasn't I who'd caused it.

"She's a real pig," he finally said after several blocks. "What the hell do I do it for? When I think of my mother or maybe a nun watching me and seeing that I could do something like that, I want to puke."

I almost wept with relief to find that the neighborhood outlaw was experiencing the same moral vertigo as I.

"Well, no one did see us," I said, happy to give comfort to someone stronger than myself.

"God saw us. Come on."

God? He could ferret us out in a basement? I looked up, saw His accusing eyes once again in the evening sky, and knew He could. I went on in silence.

Our destination proved to be St. Joan of Arc Church, to me a mysterious, forbidding building, for I knew that deep things went on inside it that I did not yet understand. When we reached the entrance, I held back. I had observed church behavior only in films, and I was apprehensive about entering this holy edifice and committing some sinful breach of spiritual protocol.

"Well, come on," Gino said.

"What are you going to do?"

"What do you think? I'm going to confession." Gino took in my blank response. "Ain't you Catholic?"

I shook my head sadly.

Gino looked thoughtfully at me for a moment, and then, anticipating his church's ecumenical era, told me that I could confess anyway. Cautiously, I walked behind him, mimicking his genuflection and gestures at the bowl of holy water, and then fell alongside him in a pew. He began praying immediately, while I looked in wonder around me. The long rectangular nave led to an altar, atop which was a silver cross bearing a tranquil Jesus. Behind this was a large lunette of colored glass that bore the stained figures of angels with threatening, agitated wings. There was no sound except the soft drone of orisons coming from the twenty or so worshipers scattered through the church. Occasionally, one of them would stir, rise and disappear into a small booth protected from view by a black curtain.

I knelt there reeking with guilt and fear, certain that I had brought the bad air of my cellar debauch with me into this place of worship. I had just discovered that life had ugly passions, and the turmoil inside me seemed stridently and offensively out of place in such a sad, quiet, waiting world, and I expected any minute that one of the priests would fasten me by the neck and send me hurtling through the door.

I wanted to get out, but even when Gino left me for the confessional, I didn't dare. There was no safety outside, and though I felt I was being smothered by the stares of saints and angels, I kept my glance fixed on the figure pinioned to wood in front of me. His clearly etched rib cage kept reminding me of Betty, and I prayed wretchedly for my own soul.

Finally Gino emerged and motioned that I was to take his place in the booth.

"What am I supposed to do?" I whispered in panic.

"Just tell him your sins, you get a penance and then you're forgiven."

"By God?"

"Jesus, you're dumb. Who else?"

I had no idea what a penance was and only a vague notion of sin, but I would risk anything for such quick pardon. I have often wondered what that silent priest thought behind his screen as he was suddenly abused by an unbroken narrative of shame and fear spiced with vivid details and rhetorical questions about the meaning of breasts and pubes. If he unraveled any meaning from my unorthodox confession, it probably left him thanking God for his vow of chastity.

When I dashed out of the church, I found Gino waiting for me.

"Well?"

"I told him everything."

"And what did he give you?"

"Give me?"

"As a penance, knobhead."

"I didn't wait, I don't know what it is."

"Christ, it don't do no good if you don't get a penance, like saying a hundred Hail Mary's."

"No good?"

"Never mind, I'll give you one myself."

"You can do it?"

"Sure, why not. Let's go on down to the five-and-dime."

My atonement was to stand guard while Gino reduced the Woolworth inventory by two hammers and a small screwdriver, and the fear of being caught was nothing compared to the relief I felt at having been so quickly shriven by my new religion. I knew that no matter how furiously I might have pleaded with my mother's nebulae and constellations, they never would have come to my aid. Unknown to the Holy See, it had gained a convert.

I remained one for as long as my role as Gino's friend lasted. We committed petty thievery together, terrified smaller boys, masturbated in unison and went every Friday night to see Betty disrobe in her cellar (I grew slowly to tolerate her body), and then on to an accounting of the week's sins. I confessed everything in my improvisational way: my fear of darkness, my wish that my father was taller, my hope for good grades at school, my desire that my mother would live forever. Wishes, deeds, fears were all indiscriminately tossed in, for, since I had no way of judging the religious value of the secrets I possessed, I spewed them all out in order that I might be certain nothing displeasing to Christ went undetected. Imitating my first success, I never once gave enough pause in my declarations for the priest to interject a query as to just what manner of Catholic I was, much less to prescribe a penance. That Gino still meted out in exciting ways, the last of which was the theft of a lady's purse. Running from her outraged screams, swinging between crime and absolution, I found the spiritual harmony I'd been searching for.

I had just about reached the point where I was going to tell my mother of my new beliefs and ask her to help me make a more formal entrance into the church when Gino tired of my company. I had somehow believed that the vagaries of his friendship would not apply to me, but suddenly he broke off a scheduled meeting we were to have to engage in some rooftop voyeurism, and the next day, at school, he avoided me. Without him, I knew I would never have the nerve to go back to that melancholy building in which I still felt alien. The thought of again being without spiritual order in my life made me hold back any pride, and I set off to visit Gino later that afternoon.

He lived on the edge of our neighborhood in a run-down house constructed of wood and gummy shingles. Vast lots surrounding it were used for improvised junkyards by the community, and the neighborhood garbage spilled over into a weedy yard that led to a collapsed and cluttered porch. When I arrived, Gino was sitting on the porch steps with his mother. Though I had glimpsed her once inside the house while waiting for her son to come out, I had never gotten a good look at her until now. From her size, there was no doubt that she could have borne Gino. Every part of her was swollen and puffed into proportions that hardly seemed human, and each movement sent her whole body rippling with flesh. Her hair was a wild, white penumbra, around a face raw with blemishes, and it wore a vacant, gap-toothed smile that had nothing to do with humor. I stopped when they saw me, and then walked tentatively toward Gino.

"What do you want?" he said in an unwelcoming voice.

"Well, I thought we could do something together."

"I'm not doin' nothin' with you no more." Gino was dull and sullen. "You give me a pain in the ass."

"You no shoulda talk to a friend that way, Gino. You no shoulda talk."

His mother's intercession made me a bit bolder.

"Come on, Gino, aren't we going to go to confession together?"

His mother started to push herself upward excitedly.

"Eh, you see Gino, hesa good boy. He wanna go to confession. You play with him."

"I'm not going to confession no more with him. He's not even Catholic."

Now his mother was standing, looking down on me from the kitchen porch. I had never seen anything so large.

"You no Catholic?"

"Well, no, but I want . . ."

"You no know about Christ's blood?"

I looked to Gino for some help, but he was staring darkly away.

"You no see the blood of the saints that come down from heaven to keep us safe?"

Before I could answer, she had turned and gone into the kitchen.

"You get out of here, Jack," Gino said, getting up quick and angry. "You betta get outta here."

I was about to, when his mother reappeared holding a tiny cup.

"You wait," she shouted to me. "You wait. I have some holy water for your head."

Sowing the water like seeds in front of her, the woman

53

flowed down the steps like an ocean. I didn't move or flinch when the drops struck me.

"Do you see the Holy Ghost?" she asked, still flicking a fine spray at me with her fingers. "I see, it's a bird, and its wings wrap around us all."

She spread her thick arms out and began to enfold me in them. I experienced the strong odor of sanctity coming from her body.

"You no send this boy to Hell. I put the water on him."

I was now lost in her flesh. I thought I would never get out of the rancid darkness I was in. I was going to die, then and there.

"Let him go!" Gino's voice came through to me and then it was light again. The woman, being pulled by her son, crashed to the ground. The strange smile was still in place. Gino was crying.

"I put the water on him. I can hear the wings. I can hear the wings."

Her voice faded away as I ran home. My mother saw that I was upset and asked what had happened.

"I just saw a crazy woman," I answered.

My mother sympathized but told me I mustn't be frightened in the future of abnormal people.

That night, in my bed, I resolved to make no more assaults upon God. Whoever He was, His domain was dangerous, and I admitted that I was too young to trespass upon it. There were years ahead of me, and I was sure some clarity would come with them. Until then, I would obey my mother, teachers and other adults and live a less frenzied religious life.

I am still where I was at eleven, bogged down between an uncharitable solar system and the fat madness of Gino's mother. But, at least now, I am used to them, and there, on the golf course in Las Vegas, I could even brood beneath what once terrified me, using it as little more than a prop in a comfortable play I'd watched myself in hundreds of times. With new resolve I went back into the casino. The next time I stepped to the tables, it would not be to sneak in twenty-dollar bets. The moment in the desert, and the memories it had stirred, made me feel that, after all, I really had little to lose and that some daring was in order.

I went to the bar, which was in full swing. Men in silk suits and white jackets stood about in loose, happy conversation. They were tanned, groomed, oiled, loud and confident, and they rattled the ice in their glasses as though the sound were a mating cry or a challenge to battle. Their ladies, perched in their tight dresses on the cocktail stools, hair piled high and stiff above them, sipped pink and green concoctions through a straw. They stared straight ahead, hardly moving, their faces pinched into dignity while they waited for some acknowledgment from the men they came with. Whenever one caught my eye, she froze and looked away, letting me know she considered my stare an insult when she was so well coiffed, dressed and escorted. I didn't know if they were local professionals, weekend dates, or actual wives—when the lower class grooms itself, it is impossible to tell—but after my third drink I wanted one.

This little stirring of desire perked me up. I had one more drink to put a firm lid on this feeling and moved about the casino. I stopped first by a blackjack table, watched for a moment, and then placed a hundred-dollar bill down as a bet.

"Now you've truly begun," I thought.

The dealer announced that there was a hundred-dollar player at the table and one of the pit bosses came over to scrutinize me. I returned him as cold a look as the bar ladies had given me, but I was pleased with his attention.

The dealer replaced my bill with chips and dealt the cards. I stood pat with twenty and won when he hit fourteen and busted. In one play the deficit was removed and I was forty dollars ahead. I won two more hundred-dollar bets and then began to seesaw up and down, but since I was always ahead, I never felt threatened. After about twenty minutes, I had won five hundred dollars at the table and decided to leave winning. Chips rattling in my pocket, I walked to the cashier's booth, often a dismal route to the request for credit that must be traversed as quickly as possible, but now a conqueror's road on which I could stroll at leisure. As I counted out my chips in front of the clerk, I sensed his annoyance at my having beaten the system he was part of and I magnanimously didn't aggravate him further by showing any pleasure. He gave me six one-hundred-dollar bills and I put them casually away and began ambling among the tables, inspecting them coolly, for a few minutes secure in victory and without need of conflict.

Then I passed the baccarat table. It was roped off, with a guard at its entrance and a sign announcing that there was a twenty-dollar minimum bet and a maximum of two thousand. There were no chips used, the players all sat with stacks of twenties and hundreds in front of them, and the reality of cash had attracted a heavy crowd that gasped and whispered every time a bundle of notes changed hands.

Where else was I meant to be? I walked toward the rope, but the guard blocked my way. For a moment I had the sinking feeling that he judged me not up to the altitude of the game, but then he looked at one of the overseers, received a permissive nod, let down the rope and admitted me into the arena.

Las Vegas baccarat is different from the European style. First, one can bet with or against the bank at any time (winning bets with the bank are taxed five percent), and then, as in chemin de fer, the shoe, from which the cards are dealt, passes from player to player. Apart from this, and the fact that the dealer never has an option to pull or stay as he does in a European casino, the game has the same goal as its Old World model: namely, getting as close to nine on two or three cards as possible.

I was given a seat between a pair of old men who were playing, judging from the money in front of them, on a medium scale. One, wearing a straw hat set back on his head, gave me a jovial welcome; the other, dour and silent, had the shoe in front of him and said nothing. Though he was the bank, he did not cover all the bets made against him; this was done by the casino. Each chair at the game had a number which corresponded to a square marked *"Bank"* and *"Player"* on the table, and it was on these that the bets were placed.

I put the six hundred dollars—five hundred and forty of which was profit—in front of me and sat back in the chair. Now that I was inside the velvet rope, I felt I wanted to take a few minutes to grow used to the tempo of the game. I ordered a drink from a waitress in a tiny skirt and mesh stockings, and sat back, relishing my calm in the midst of the agitation.

I looked at the other players. Opposite me was a woman in her fifties with a round, sagging face darkened by sun and brightened by red and blue daubings, her arms clanging with bracelets. The only other players were two oily young men playing in consort, betting heavily, not doing well, asking for repeated checks on their remaining credit. Finally, perched above the game, in a chair from which one might judge a tennis match, was a hard, weary-looking man forever watching. There were two freshly scrubbed young croupiers on hand to take care of the money, and one to manipulate the wooden spatula that bore the players' cards on to the one making the largest bet against the bank. These were the personae around me.

By the time the drink arrived the shoe had left my neighbor and moved on. I took one sip and bet two hundred dollars against the bank, which had been held through four coups by the lady facing me. She drew from the box vigorously, her jewels ringing accompaniment to the cards' debut on the table. Carried high on the thin board of the croupier, they were delivered to me. I let them rest an instant, then picked both up: jack of diamonds, eight of clubs! Only the woman's having a natural nine on two cards would beat them. Not wanting to assume a victory, I forced myself to remain anxious as I displayed my cards to the table. The lady had not yet looked at hers, and the croupier turned them over. They were not close to winning, and two hundred-dollar bills were whisked my way.

I let the four hundred ride.

The bank had now passed to the pair of young men. Between them they counted out one thousand dollars for their bet. From their looks and gabble, they were in general retreat, and I felt very much in the right rhythm being against them.

I had a seven on two cards and stood pat; they drew to a three, did not improve, and one of them angrily bounced the cards across the table. I felt embarrassed by this display, hesitated for a moment, and then took my winnings off the board and leaned back in my chair. I wanted those two harassed human beings to have a play without facing the fortress of my good luck; and more, feeling as if I were in flight and had just executed a whirling, intricate maneuver, I wanted to cruise peacefully for a moment before testing myself again. I was happily drugged with my success and certain that it would continue for a while. I needed only not to break the rhythm with any analysis. I would be the perfect instinctual man, giving myself up to the flow of inspiration, neither criticizing nor tallying the results. I had gotten in the first blow so there was a chance that I was not going to be ignominiously squashed without a battle. Indeed, I was a little amazed that this advantage had been given me, for all along I had feared that, as with so much of my past life, I might be forced to catch up after an initial calamity, and that thus weighted down by intimations of frailty, I would have to struggle simply to get even.

The man next to me had a long, jovial run at the bank and then the shoe was passed to my square. I placed a hand on it as though to cement a bargain and bet four hundred dollars. After a breath, I drew the cards out as quickly as possible. They were swept up and handed to the Jeremiah-like figure next to me, who glanced at them sourly and then threw them, face up, into the center of the table. The flow was stopped: he had a natural nine.

I tossed my cards in as casually as I could, trying to keep the hope that I might match him from showing. I don't remember what my total was except that it did not win. I passed the shoe on and with the same gesture bet a second four hundred dollars. It was a thoughtless bet, but I had still no wish to fall back upon careful tactics when but a few seconds ago I'd felt I had a secret access to the hidden design of this baccarat game. The Old Testament figure next to me was now the banker. He brought the cards out slowly and deliberately, as though they were to demonstrate some doleful hypothesis. Our struggle was brief and deadly: I was forced to draw to a three and pulled an eight which reduced my count to one; he began with two tens, a baccarat, and then drew a winning seven.

This sobered me. It was not after all going to be one blessed ascent. For a moment I was angry that I had been permitted to soar for so short a time, but I quickly pulled

59

myself together. If toil was required, then I would toil, for I still sensed I was at a winning table. I went into my wallet and drew out an honest, laboring bet of twenty dollars, a sum which, an hour before, I had considered too timid for my plans.

In three cold, cautious hours the twenty dollars, under my husbanding, spiraled into three thousand, the last two of which came to me during five straight wins with the bank. When the shoe had been passed on, I sat for a time staring at the money in front of me. I had never been more certain of achievement in my life and I felt the satisfying, giddy fatigue that follows all worthwhile labor. This was what I had wanted. I had won myself the beginning of a world, and in gratitude I tipped each of the croupiers fifty dollars, got up from the table and watched my fellow players fade away, mired in their commonplace fortunes.

I had left the casino in a hallowed and overwhelmed frame of mind. In my room, however, I fell into an orgy of exultation. I spread the hundred-dollar bills upon the bed and walked around and around them, staring at this evidence of my success, my charm, my new self-definition. How I wished that all the eyes that had watched me through the night, all the clear, pitying eyes of the past, were there now, focused on my spoils and my joy. No miser on being told that not only could he take his wealth with him after death but could also purchase with it a better eternity, could have felt more rapture at the sight of hard currency than I did then. Let it go on, I thought, and I will fill every moment of life with well-considered pleasures. I'll not boast, strut, or demand my likeness to be put on public walls. If what I feel now can continue unclouded, then for all time count me a happy man.

I turned on the radio and, as I put the money carefully away, danced to a soft bossa nova. Then into the shower where I washed off the nervous resin that had coated my body through the evening. Without drying, I put on a robe and lay across the bed. While the air cooled me, I looked down at my body and, feeling it was again important to hold on to youth, tightened the muscles in my stomach and drew it down to a flat plane. I laughed at this but was happy to see the problems of vanity were back in my life.

I looked at my traveler's clock. It was nearly one in the morning. Soon a small favor to myself would arrive via the bell captain, and when she did, it would be to attend one with no dark needs or complicated whims. That night, everything, even my oldest desires, was clear, simple and marked for an easy success.

Chapter III

I have always kept up a good commerce with whores, but never so much as when I started to gamble. This was not, I stress, due to gambling's having a fierce aphrodisiac core. Just the opposite: I could sit, as I did, in one of New York's more interesting saloons, encased in the structure of a poker game, and stare only with a removed, unbiased pleasure at the lean young girls of our age, girls whom nature and fashion have conspired to make the happiest examples of healthy proportion since the species began. With cool wonder, I watched their rumps undulating beneath fashionable pants and dresses, and all that stirred in me was a general esthetic glow, a warm, vague appreciation of the living creatures who formed a background for the excitement and agony of the cards in front of me. I had, after all, entered a world of demanding renunciation, and no promising glance, no inviting twist to the features of these exquisite creatures could get me up from the table if there was still another card or hand to be played. I had discovered the cold, pure enjoyment of being encapsulated in something of deep meaning and demand, and I was at last comprehending the force that had kept a Humboldt in search of another specimen, a Goethe another line, a Caesar another province. It is, after all, our compulsions which turn us into great men.

But the whores? Well, they were simply there, as they have always been in my life, waiting in attendance. It was to them that I had long ago entrusted my first desires, and although at this time that may seem a quaint practice, I must plead that the neighborhood in which I grew up did not in any way anticipate the sexual carnival we enjoy today. Then, there seemed only two types of women to choose from: Irish Catholics and Italian Catholics, and both were glum objects to dally with. How I remember the Irish: their long, hollow-chested torsos bent forward as they slouched by scuffing loafered and bobby-soxed feet along the pavement; their pale, watery eyes and lacteal, pimply skin; their pinched, inchoate features—in all, the petulant aspect of the Gaelic virgin, who so often looks as if she is in a deep menstrual brood for thirty days of each month. As for the Italians, you could, for the most part, color them a shade darker than their Irish sisters and leave it at that. There were, of course, a few who enjoyed glandular explosions during the seventh and eighth grades, but their unabashed ripeness was too much for someone like myself, someone whose masturbatory dreams still sought a prepubescent angularity in their casts. Besides, these Mediterranean girls always seemed to have a shadowy escort of watchful, unhumorous relatives, and, over all their precocious sexual flamboyance, there hung a cloud of heavy Neapolitan domesticity. As an example, there was a sweet, plump *ragazza* called Tina Spagnolo who lived on my street, who always wore starched white dresses to set off her olive skin, and with whom I had been flirting for a month in a sulky, teen-aged manner. Finally, one quiet summer afternoon, she let me know that I had been accepted as a boyfriend and, after we had adjourned to a vacant lot to kiss, she invited me solemnly to her house. I didn't know exactly what to expect from this invitation but what I found was some fifteen relatives, clustered in the chiaroscuro of a tiny, airless parlor, weeping over a coffin in which Tina's uncle lay supporting a little pyramid of flowers on his chest. Tina led me up to the corpse, cried a little, and then squeezed my hand.

Suddenly, the body of the dead uncle didn't bother me nearly so much as the heavy rhythm of family life around me, the life which, even in my biological ignorance, I sensed Tina kept hidden in her womb. Stretched out among the sobs and shadows of that parlor was a living tedium more frightening than any death I could imagine, and this was too great a price to pay for the rough fondle of an ensweatered breast—the going token of affection at the time. I nodded rudely to the mourners as I went outside to take in great gulps of air, and I did not turn back when I heard Tina calling me.

There were of course those other girls, demented atrocities like Betty who lay impassively in boiler rooms, behind schoolyard handball walls, or in the sand traps of the nearby golf course while a group of us would swagger our way through a gangbang; but while these events helped me to adjust to a more mature female anatomy, my retarded place in the line and the catatonic expression on these girls' faces usually made me retire after a few soft, unpenetrating efforts.

No, the first woman really to lead me through the tunnel was a professional. Her name was Jane Polanski. How old she was, I cannot remember, except that to me, then, she appeared well along into adult blossom. She was large, blonde, full-breasted, with a quiet, open face that betokened resignation rather than any wild passion. When I met her, she was wearing a blue satin dress slit along the sides, and, with her co-workers, was leaning stoically over the guardrail which encircled a half-empty dance floor. She was a hostess in the Samba Palace, one of those old benighted dance halls and places of rendezvous along Broadway, and I, flush with Christmas money, was in from the sticks of Jackson Heights looking for big-city thrills. We danced, I bought her Coca-Colas at a dollar a glass and cigarettes at a dollar a package. With a pleasant tenacity, which consisted of a grind or two while we danced and some whispered obscenities while we were at table, she coaxed me to such extravagance that, in less than an hour, strands of dance tickets dangled from her like confetti. Our first meeting ended with my having just enough money left to uncheck my overcoat and command a subway home. But I also took with me a promise that the next time we met, if I could arrive nearer to the four o'clock closing time with thirty-five dollars, there would be rewards greater than abdominal bumps to a foxtrot tempo. I looked into her bored, ingenuous *Mitteluropa* face, a face transmitting the features of generations of one-night stands in taverns along the roads between Warsaw and Budapest, and, though I really had no choice, I trusted her.

A few days later, this confidence was rewarded. Jane, smelling of powder and a strong, peppermint perfume, gave me a mediocre launching into manhood in the sadly furnished rented room of a two-family house, oddly enough just a few blocks from where I lived at the time. I say mediocre perhaps unjustly: Jane was competent and patient, permitting me all sorts of curious investigations and helping me without laughter or condescension through the choreography of an honest, aboveboard screw. There was not much excitement in her, however, for she claimed the subway ride had tired her out and that she'd been unusually mangled and trod upon by the night's customers. Dumbly, I had had to wait while, for twenty minutes, she rubbed and soaked her swollen feet, and maintained a grim silence broken only by heavy, working-class sighs.

Nevertheless, I remember afterward walking the streets at dawn, the first time I had ever been up at that hour without sleep, happily inhaling the female odors that still clung to my clothes. In terms of pleasure, depressions, horrors and delights, I was confused, but I did feel keenly satisfied and part of the larger world of heroes and adventure that I was impatiently waiting to explore. Jane had provided a little human blessing for the journey, and I was still grateful to her when, a decade later, long after she had ceased her bovine hustle at the Samba Palace, I saw her picture still festooning its entrance, fixing her as she was in 1949, in a broad-shouldered gown, a rosebud mouth, and a rush of curly blond hair spilling well over her shoulders. The photograph gave prominence to the first breasts I had actually fondled at leisure, and, passing by, now a sexual veteran, I looked at them warmly, wondered at the rush of time, and saluted their honest, hardworking, Polish-born owner.

Many followed Jane, but, as I said, with gambling my play with whores swelled to the extent of tri-weekly orgies occasioned by an early-morning wish to tear open the sheath of tension which the night's play had wrapped around me. But there were deeper reasons too, reasons that spun about the need to step back for a moment from the unremitting data of wins and losses, from the precise addition of my self's worth of an evening, from the ritualized sayings, grumbles and exultations of other gamblers; in short, to dip for a moment into a weaker, more ill-defined, more human world, a world which did not demand that one's secrets be turned up continually, which allowed pretensions to replace calculations, and which encouraged foolishness, illusion, and the sort of grand, tawdry lies that one creates for strangers while on vacation. These 5:00 A.M. treks were brief holidays from the austere pleasures which defined all that I had discovered important about myself. If I had behaved and worked well, if I had not suffered a numbing loss, then I might indulge my frailties with a short, secular tour through the environs of Forty-second Street, gathering up two or three hookers desperate for some rewarding score before the day's commuters erupted from the subways and stifled, with morning papers and Nedick's orange juice, the nighttime atmosphere of search and sell. And so I would arrive for the last shift, as expansive as a conventioneer, offering more money than the girls would probably make in three nights of ordinary, moody, suspicious tricks, insinuating, in an over-excited babble, that I had strange desires, and that together we could hold back the sun, have a *bal masqué*, make a swinging scene.

"You a cop?" was generally their first response (I never did understand why they considered exuberance and hyperbole attributes of the vice squad), and at this I would then tone myself down and return to the enticing business of money. Soon I would have their dark faces showing that tiny bit of trust which was all these ladies needed to make them risk thirty days in jail or disembowelment at the hand of a sexual extremist.

Finally, we would be off to my apartment, and the early mornings were full of music and the cackles of Geraldines, Gigis, Ronnies and Bobbies as, under my command, they pranced about the living room and arranged themselves into

67

various black tableaux, giggling and slipping, trying earnestly to match my whims, and vying with each other for personal attention which might call for an extra tip.

"What you see in that Gigi?" Ronnie would say. "She got a black, ugly face that look like forty mile uh bad road."

"Hey, Jack," Geraldine whispers, "that Ronnie ain't gonna give you nothin'. She ain't got the chops for what you want. Now I got an ass on me like uh Mississippi mule. You can bang away till *you* get tired."

And now Bobbie insinuates herself while feigning a search for a glass in my kitchen: "Sheet, we can make somethin' happen, baby, you git rid of them two dragass whores. I' know the kinda scene you lookin' for. You want to have it all your way, don't you, Colonel? That's cool with me."

It was high court intrigue, but I generally kept them serving equally while, hunched on all fours, their magnificent bottoms pointing skywards to receive my restrained promptings, they paraded proudly as I tried to draw the folds of my mind further and further apart so that any new, happy excess could easily violate it. It was as if I wanted to parody carnal pleasure, to make of it some grotesque, comical Sancho next to the quixotic exultations of my gambling. It was a burlesque orgy, and I let my pale, flaccid body hover like a spirit over the swarm of blackness at its feet. At times I wanted these dark women to rise up, rip, flay and quarter me; but then I would remember that I, too, still had a small coal of desire worth fanning with a little more breath, the desire to catch my fate in some sparkling baroque casino and finally to be, like the civilization for which my white body stood surrogate, remembered for a Faustian arrogance.

Yes, there were high moments, but the morning saturnalias never lasted for more than an hour. I simply could not sustain them. Something always would break into the mood, some moment of aperceptive intolerance would snatch the joy from the game and I would be left with the simple, straightforward business of achieving a quick, tepid coming in the midst of an ebony flurry of breasts and thighs. Sometimes the end of the imaginative play would be caused by a book set out upon the coffee table, a book that would remind me that, after all, I had a sobering intelligence; sometimes it would be an unreal and unexpected flash of myself in the reflection of a mirror; sometimes my gums would simply start to bleed; and often it was my downstairs neighbor, a professor of art history at a girls' college in New York, who would call pleading for rest before he rose to go and explain the significance of Merovingian ornaments to his students.

Whatever the pall, the girls sensed it immediately, and while one of them worked on me with professional speed, the others would be hastily climbing into their shreds of underwear, straightening their wigs, adjusting seams and eyelashes, and in female ways preparing to meet an Eastside morning between Fifth and Madison Avenues—for them, not the easiest of confrontations.

And then they were gone. *Avant peur de mourir lorsque je couche seul,* said Mallarmé, excusing a late-night preoccupation with whores or poetry. With me, *au contraire,* I would be certain of death if the Gigis, Geraldines or any other stranger wanted to stretch out beside me and share the intimacies of sleep, intimacies which I find more personally obliterating than any sexual exchange. Nothing, I believe, so splinters the self as a bed shared with an unknown body. To hear, on the verge of unconsciousness, alien sighs, scratches and groans makes me suspect that my very thoughts may not be mine. I feel then that there is no substance to me at all, that the temporary oblivion I'm about to experience is abstract and total. Therefore, if I have one area of brute, visceral discrimination, it is in the care with which I try to select someone of trusted quality and compassion to doze next to, someone who will let me move into dreams with my secrets hoarded together for my own selfish sleep.

No, I was never sorry to see the whores depart. A fresh silence would slip into my rooms and I would feel, left alone, peculiarly comfortable with the idiosyncrasies of the last night. There was, of course, now and then a small spasm of fear as I got into bed, fear that, with the frenzies of gambling and my high-spirited black whores, I had broken irrevocably away from the comfortable orbit of a rational life. And then, too, there would be a whiff of educated anxiety over the purpose and design behind all the risks I was taking. Still, my life had now become intense enough to mute these buzzings, and, like a sighing Cavalier poet, pleased with his own sensibility, I would go off to sleep hanging in a sweet agony between post-coital depression and post-Copernican despair.

But now, in Las Vegas, a three-thousand-dollar victory tucked beneath a mound of socks in my suitcase, I felt little need of the morning bacchanals that had calmed me in New York. I had begun my journey, the first trial had been passed, and if I had asked the bell captain—the sweet, respectful smile he gave me!—for a woman, it was meant only as a deprecation of any godlike feelings, a gentle *homo es.*

The soft bossa nova bounced off my room's pastel walls, ice tinkled gloriously in my glass, my body luxuriated in the silk robe that covered it, and, from my window, I looked down upon the Strip, watching cars flash by beneath the colossal lights of the hotels, which, in infinite varieties of colored script, wrote images of the American desert in the sky—*Sands, Dunes, Golden Nugget*—names in mammoth swirls of neon that kept darkness forever outside the city limits. I saluted all that I could see with a sip from my glass, and then my doorbell, an octave-spaced chime, softly rang.

If there is anything wrong about her, I thought, I'll pay up and send her away. Everything's too perfect now to put up with a badly turned breast or a mustached upper lip.

I opened the door and the evening continued a triumph. There, in the portal, was a blond creature of about eighteen, with a face as lasciviously drowsy as a Balthus child's. She was all golden, in a yellow dress, wearing yellow shoes, and, most touching of all, carrying a tiny yellow purse. With refrigerated blue eyes, she took a quick, knowing appraisal of me and then smiled at the happy simplicity she must have caught in my mood.

"You seem to be havin' a party all by yourself," she said in a sharp, metallic drawl. I had heard those twanging sounds before, long ago, during the stretched-out, torturous Army days at Camp Chaffee, Arkansas.

"You're an Arkansan?" I asked, as she glanced around the room to make certain that we were to be *à deux*.

"Close," she said, frowning a bit, probably over the fact that I had anticipated part of her standard conversational give-and-take. As a rule, whores ask questions, and seem generally perplexed or uninterested when, in return, a little social interrogation is required of them. "I'm from Oklahoma," she added finally, and then, with a proper crossing of legs, sat down daintily in one of the chairs. "Fort Sill. I've been in Arkansas a lot."

From an Oklahoma Army town to Las Vegas—the route of escape. She must have realized at an early age that she was several cuts above the ordinary camp follower and had moved on—here, to the air-conditioned refinement of a gambler's suite. I thought of those I had seen like her around Army bases; wives in slacks and wedgies, their hair eternally condemned to curlers, pushing prams and shopping carts about the P.X., young girls already puffed of face from matching their non-commissioned husbands' drinking habits, always smoking, chattering, and pulling a hazy, transient life together that had begun on a three-day pass spent in the boozy marvel of a motel. I thought of those girls, how they stiffened sullenly whenever an officer's wife glided by them in the commissary, and I was glad this little whore had run away to Las Vegas.

Now she was settling into the room, slowly, obviously getting ready for some humanizing talk before discussing bed and board. I went to make us a drink, and from the angle of the bar got to peek at her at leisure. Exquisite! Pert, compact, with fierce little breasts and slim, round calves and thighs. I have mentioned Balthus, and her face did have his charming insinuation of evil running through its baby features, but the more I stared, the more Crivelli came to mind, Crivelli of the golden lady caught in a frame of peacocks and heavy, ripe, joyful fruit. But finally she was very much my Lady of America—half Oklahoma Gothic, half Las Vegas voluptuousness.

"My name's Sally. What's yours?"

I told the truth. Usually, at this moment, at this question, I would fall into glorious lies. "Winfield Scott," "Sebastian David," "Johnny Laredo"—these had been some of my aliases stretching back to the Samba Palace, a pseudonymous trail of caution, suspicion, nominal discontent and cinema romance. But now I spoke my proper name out clearly.

"From the way you're flyin' around here, it looks like you won some money tonight."

Pride and discretion did battle within me.

"Yes, I won."

"Hey, that's real nice now," Sally laughed, squirming out of the chair and beginning an excited march around the

72

room. "The trouble always comes from losers who feel that the town now owes them something free. They want to bitch the price with me an' I don't like bitchin'. The old men are the worst. The ones with the cigars and little silk suits. Haven't *seen* it in ten years and then want me to get it up fer 'em in seconds. Then they *still* bitch about the price."

Her complaint, I admit, was crude, but I loved the serious outrage and tone with which it was delivered. She rambled on about the curiosities and trials of her business, and I did nothing more than nod sympathetically from a stretched-out position on the bed. Years of difficulties with lovely girls of a simple, direct nature like Sally's had taught me that there is something about my style of conversation that upsets them, something that makes them draw back coolly from my metaphors and turns of phrase as if they were insulting obscenities. I generally consoled myself by assuming that any form of figurative language must seem a mode of insanity to the semiliterate, but this was poor comfort when, after having burst out with a rich, imaginative paragraph, I found myself being written off simply as another creep. I didn't want one of those quizzical, cold smiles coming from Sally, so I avoided as much as possible the dangers of language, mumbling only an agreement here and there to punctuate her list of complaints. Then, finally, came a silence, the traditional little interim that always hangs between the amenities of a first-class hooker and the moment of business. She was standing at the foot of the bed, staring down at me, her arms in a determined fold.

"Well, what did you have in mind, Jack?"

Was willst du, Schatz? Qu'est-ce que tu veux, chéri? ¿Qué deseas, querido? I had certainly heard the question before, in rooms over the Trocadero in Frankfurt as a soldier, in the tiny, functional hotels off Place Clichy, in the cribs of the *zonas rojas* in Mexico. And it was a question I could never really answer, for when asked for an honest confession of my wishes, a mushroom cloud of savage needs would spread out in my brain, but it was always made up of indistinct, formless gyrations of flesh that refused to coalesce into a specific answer. Whores had long since taught me that what I considered to be my black secrets of carnal excess were, in fact, tired commonplaces easily categorized for fast and simple dispatch, and it was not therefore any clinical embarrassment which clogged my mind. Perhaps the question was too much for my imagination to hold for a simple answer, since, so often, from the base of my mind, I would hear a rumbling, inarticulate response which called darkly on these ladies to obliterate me with pleasure, and there is no precise expression for this except a dryly spoken "Everything."

"Everything?" Sally frowned. "What does that mean?"

I sensed a fissure creeping through our rapport, and I answered with a weak, inconclusive gesture of my hand.

"All I do is straight and French," Sally said, her voice now a little wary but, to me, still warmly seductive. Ah, Sally, I thought, I will be as straight as you desire. And if you want to exalt the French by giving them exclusive synonymity with oral delights, I will not chauvinistically protest. Tonight I have won so much that an idyllic, rather than a dramatic, lay will suffice.

"That's fine," I said. "That's all I do, too; that's all I ever do."

Sally nodded understandingly. "But," she said, "we've got something to discuss first."

I nodded. Let us speak the numbers and get it over with.

"A hundred dollars."

The figure stunned me. No matter how time or wars or the moods of commerce inflate, devalue, or make other economic rearrangements with currency, "one hundred" will always have for me an impressive and intimidating sound. "One hundred"—when I was growing up, this was what was needed, as a weekly wage, to be rich, or, at least, to provide passage from Queens to one of the marvelous towers that stood serenely across the river. Faced with a hundred-dollar expense, I always have to remind myself that the financial rules have changed and that the once formidable figure of Depression psychology has been reduced to a humble arithmetical unit without any special social glamour.

"A hundred dollars? That for the night?"

"No, Jack, you know better than that. This is Vegas. It's a hundred a pop."

I wanted to celebrate and felt relaxed and pre-potent. Indeed, mulling over Sally's attributes, I had anticipated between three and four decently spaced pops before dawn. But to spend a tenth of my winnings on these comings seemed prohibitive at even decadent rates of exchange. Fifty-dollar tips to the croupiers were one thing, for that is an expected part of the ritual of winning. But to pay out a hundred dollars for each spasm! I am not cheap or thrifty, but gambling had invested money with the quality of a medium necessary to the conditions of life. It was not that I wanted to *do* anything with it, any more than I wanted to *do* something with oxygen or sunlight; it was simply that cash had become the element I needed for my personal evolution. Vestigial, lower-order desires occasionally made me squander a little of this precious substance, but a firm sense of self-preservation helped me recoil from indiscriminate popping at the prices Sally quoted, and so I stayed silent, forcing her to present some alternatives.

"If you're going to be here awhile," she said, "we could work out somethin' so I stay with you. You know, go to dinner and the shows and all."

With the meter running all the while? Hardly. I wanted

to leave the subject, make the arrangement, keep the en-
chantment of the night moving along at a gallop. I had
already, at the last proposal, begun noticing a tiny flaw in
Sally's beauty: her hair, while pretending to a straight, loose,
Alice-in-Wonderland fall to her shoulders, had been frozen
by some evil spray into an unhuman rigidity. When she
nodded, hair and head moved all of a piece. If this bar-
gaining continued, I felt more defects might appear.

On the table next to me was my wallet. From it I took a
hundred-dollar bill and presented it to Sally, indicating
which of her buying plans had interested me. I expected
her to look disappointed, but without fuss she snapped the
money into her purse, sent me a naughty reproach with her
eyes when I groped for her, and went off to the bathroom to
prepare her pre-coital toilet.

I stretched out on the bed and waited. This was an interim which I had grown used to since the advent of inti-
mate hygiene and devilish gadgets to ward off conception.
One no longer coaxed and wheedled a woman into bed,
there to have her in a swirl of unconsidered passion. No,
now, at the moment when Molly Bloom said "yes," at the
instant when the dark declivities are moist and ready, there
comes a whispered entreaty for patience and the heavy
clump of footsteps in the darkness as the lady slips away to
her bathroom laboratory. It is a dangerous moment, for one
is left alone with sagging erectile tissue and rising doubts
about enjoying the upcoming sexual tumble. Indeed, one
starts to wonder if it is all really worth even the effort of taking off and putting on clothes in a strange surrounding, and
when this is pondered, something peculiar inevitably happens: there is a realization, as one sees one's body rising
evenly with each breath and stretched out, white and vulnerable, in the darkness, that roles have been oddly re-
versed, that he who has hunted and stalked with such dis-

cretion has, in fact, been teased into a trap, and that the muffled, female toilet sounds betoken a coming rite in which he will play an ignominious role. At this moment, one feels no more than a flesh-and-blood dildo, or an expendable tribesman spread out and waiting for a sacrificial knife.

Sally was back before I slipped too deeply into these reflections, and with her she carried the ordnance of the moment; two enormous pool towels and a warm wet facecloth. But behind these, she was naked, and her body, made even smaller now by the absence of her two-inch-heeled shoes, was one compact, inviting muscle, a dimpled hardness made for quick, sensual reflexes.

She set the towels aside and, after a quick check for any inflammation of the genital tract, began to wipe and massage my groin with the warm, damp, pink washcloth. This was a professional prologue that I had once found nettling, but I had, years ago, during my days in the Army, used my imagination to color and soften the clinical mood of the scene: Lieutenant Richardson, suffering from a vicious shrapnel wound in the groin, his precious parts mutilated but still held together as if by a virile act of will, being ministered to by Nurse Sally, virgin, but with a woman's inborn acceptance of the raw physicalities of life, who will attend the bloodied shreds of his body until they are whole, healthy and capable of offering her their gratitude, which she will of course blushingly accept.

Finally, I am clean and pure enough for us to begin. Sally lowers lights, and curls about me, angling herself into position to discharge the Gallic part of her duties. Then, a pleasant wave swells through my body, and I place my head snugly between her calves, close my eyes and reflect on the good fortune that had brought this charming whore into my bed. For this entwinement with Sally I considered a piquant example of all the uncomplicated pleasures I might

77

finally have if I could, through gambling, escape once and for all from the mental labyrinth in which I had so long confined myself. Not that there hadn't been a certain comfort in its winding corridors, in the twists and turnings of thought, memory, and reflection. But I had long since grown weary of being a spectator even to my own couplings, a fastidious observer who found the positions of love a little absurd and who even at the climax of passion could not fully escape from his own totalitarian solitude.

Though I knew we were whore and client, I felt Sally and I were more than two contiguous bits of aloneness. I had won three thousand dollars—the sound of that number, its long vowel and fierce diphthong, rang delight through me each time I spoke it to myself—and, on command, Sally had appeared to celebrate my entering a world of chance and sensuality. She was scratching at my outer wall, a whisper inviting me to stay with my quest.

"You got your mind on business, Jack?" Sally asked suddenly. "I'm not gettin' much action down here."

"What do you do, Sally," I asked, "when you are going down on some particularly old and ugly man?"

"What?" .

"I mean, what do you think of?"

Sally laughed a little. "I don't think of anything. If there's a mirror nearby, I make faces at myself. You know, I cross my eyes and puff out my cheeks, things like that. Just to remind me what a fool I'm diddlin' with."

"And," I asked slowly, "were you making faces just now?"

Sally seemed really hurt. "Was that how it was coming through to you? Maybe I'm no good at it then, maybe I'm no good at all."

"No," I consoled her, "you were fine. I was just wondering a little, that's all."

78

"Well, stop wonderin' and put your mind to things. I wouldn't never make any faces with you."

I smiled and gently palmed her head, forcing it back down to its agreeable duties. Indeed, my mind wasn't sternly on business and, in a slow, self-satisfied way, it still was meandering. Sally, for all her charm, did not help to fix my attention on the moment, for she had one of those abstractly beautiful bodies, bodies without particular twists or markings, which, when scanned leisurely, recall to me all the past pleasures that I've drawn from female recesses in general. I thought then, or perhaps now with Sally's flanks lighting up my mind, back to my first hooker, back to solemn, placid Jane who had once, with the enthusiasm of a peasant kneeling to pray, done to me in her furnished Jackson Heights room what Sally was now doing above the Las Vegas desert. (First love, first kiss, first fellatio—the times change and the styles of growing up with them.) Jane, too, had referred to this act as "doing a French" and had added that only because I was young and clean was she offering me this special favor. I am still grateful for that judgment, and I think of Jane, Sally and me, a trio ever young, ever clean, and ever American, off on a wicked holiday among alien perversions. *Tu m'as fait un bon pompier*, Sally. *Et, toi aussi*, Jane, *tu sais comment faire une bonne pipe.* Let us hide in the language of those you believed responsible for the advent of such evil deeds.

And now into this calm erotica a memory of my mother, a woman more worldly in her imaginings than either Jane or Sally. It is the day after my Polish conquest and I see her appearing with the pants I had worn the night before draped over her arms. Before exploding into my room, she

79

had obviously set her face in a reproachful grimace, but there was too much merriment around her mouth and eyes to be caged in by affected seriousness. I knew the expression well; it meant that I had done something which demanded a conventional maternal condemnation, but over which her imagination was secretly pleased. For an eternal minute she stood before me, dangling the pants daintily between her forefinger and thumb, relishing, with her blue, gleaming eyes, my uneasiness.

"What on earth is this, Jackie?" she asked finally, and her smile insinuated that she knew everything and that she just wanted to be, as she was in so much else, the first sharer of my secrets. But the pants? What had the pants to do with anything? I stared and stared at them, but could find no damning evidence of debauch until, suddenly, along the inside lining of the fly, I glimpsed blotches of lipstick, shameless, rose-colored smudges that ran the entire length of the zipper. I cursed Jane's sloppy manners and pretended to see nothing.

"What do you mean 'what is this?'" I asked, looking intently at the crotch of my pants. "I don't see anything." I had always been frank with my mother about my early sexual discoveries, and she, in her romantic way, had always been so with me. She, not my father, had explained the functions of passion to me, using phrases like "and then the body trembles," "fluid explodes out of you," "you tingle with a sense of pleasure and life." But it seemed a long way from these refulgent images to Jane's cosmetic smears along the inner lining of a pair of Botany pants.

"Jackie, Jackie, Jackie"—three long sighs of bemused exasperation, as if I had again gone and provided her with an example of my marvelous, genius-indicating specialness— "I know what this lipstick means. Now tell me, and be honest, did this come off any of the girls I know?"

Now it was my turn to tease, to keep her suspended. I mumbled, muttered, pretended embarrassment and ignorance; she smiled, sighed, fluttered the pants nervously and pleaded now for frankness between us. Then, just as we reached an hysterical pitch in our playing, I began to blurt the story out.

Halfway through the details, I realized I had made some profound error in judgment. The wonder and amusement dissolved from my mother's face and were replaced by a sour anger, a resentful, pinched disappointment.

"You paid this woman, Jackie?"

As soon as this had been icily said, I knew what was wrong. Once, several years before, I had come home from a birthday party in delirious contentment and informed her that the acknowledged beauty of the class had chosen me as her partner for a bout of necking in a bedroom closet. My triumph was met with stiff, injured pride, and then I was curtly told that she was actually sickened by how obviously little I thought of myself. *Her* son should not be set off into spins of bumpkinish wonder because he had soul-kissed a twelve-year-old. On the contrary, I was the one who had performed the favor, and what she expected to see in the future was the cool smile of someone who is certain that, for him, women were disposable packages of enjoyment. My cretinous smile was a breach of the rakehell heritage she believed in for her son and a betrayal of the fine profile she had bequeathed me—the long, angular, nervous profile which she insisted was aristocratic. After that event, she had sulked for days, letting drop acid prophecies that I would, with my excessive humility, end up marrying the janitor's daughter—a fat, myopic creature with Mongoloid features and no saliva control—the first time she wetly grinned at me.

But now, of course, what I had done was infinitely worse. I had paid money for what was, in my mother's mind, a divine right. I had not seduced, I had not been a gay magnet that by its nature drew to it trembling female bodies. No, I had paid, paid like any clod out on a Saturday night. It was too much for her. She let the pants slip disdainfully to the floor, rose from the bed, and stared down at me with eyes filled with grief. My mother often cried when reality disappointed her, and it had just done so.

"You . . . you . . . you take those pants to be cleaned, Jackie. I want nothing more to do with them."

I tried to protest, but she would have none of it.

"No . . . no"—she was looking past me, at some vision which sustained her in such bad moments—"let's drop this subject. I'm going in now to take down the Christmas tree. It's time. The needles are beginning to fall. Yes, it's time to take it down."

I was desperate. To leave it at this would mean months of such wistfulness, months of listening to long, sad accusing sighs. I tried one last defense. "But Van Gogh went to prostitutes," I said. "You know he did. We read about it together." At the time, he was my mother's favorite painter, the very symbol of art and imagination. Reading to me from a popular biography of the Dutchman, she would stop and marvel over his agony, genius, and dramatic, haphazard life. I had come to understand that he was part of that vision she saw whenever our small Queens apartment became too oppressive.

For a moment, I thought I had hit the mark. I saw her waver, stitching her emotions together carefully. But then, just as she left the room: "Van Gogh was tormented, Jackie. Are you tormented?"

She closed the door and I was alone. "Tormented"—my mother had spoken the word dreamily, as though to achieve the state it described meant an absolution from all human grossness. I pondered and stared at the objects spread about my room—a small desk, two homemade bookcases, a heavy red-leather club chair passed on to me by a dead uncle, two lithographs depicting London markets at the time of Mayhew. Everything seemed flat, ordinary and comfortable, definitely not the paraphernalia of torment. But there were times at night, in a brief waking interlude between dreams, when my things had seemed marvels of strangeness, contorted perfections of the fear that had startled me awake. Tormented? I might be, I thought. I might honestly be. And if I wasn't? Well, then I would become so if it meant inspiring my mother and excusing the whims I had about the way I wished to live. God, yes—for I was already planning other visits to Jane—I could make myself tormented.

Sally stopped and glanced back over her shoulder. Like a child with no one to play with, she was frowning moodily.

"I'm wastin' my time," she chided.

I felt very foolish, for I was letting the cap to the evening slip away into abstractions and memories.

"I love you, Sally," I said loudly, and before she could undercut me with a hard, whorish riposte, I repeated the phrase three more times and then dove down to hide between her thighs. There, among labia major and minor, I savored for the first time the ointment that she had put on minutes before. I could not believe the signals my tastebuds were sending to my brain. Strawberry! A strawberry-flavored, genuine American piece of sexual confection. It was more than human; it was the ambrosial cunnilingus of the Olympians; it was the transformation that luck and fortune can make even of the flesh.

And Sally and I made love, neatly and classically, within the categories of our contract. The shade of my mother may have sighed moodily, for, after nearly twenty years, I was still lying with whores, paying (two pops' worth it would prove to be) like a low-bred salesman for a little action on the road. Still, her spectre may have fluttered with some pride over the cool quality of the moment and the fact that her son had gambled his way into it. At least, with the knowledge of the dead, she would see that I had had my necessary torments and that, to honor our old visions, I was still trying to be exceptional.

Chapter IV

Morning makes a timid entrance into Las Vegas, insinuating itself with silver modesty among the thousand-watt spires, signs and billboards, waiting until the master switches of the hotels are thrown, until the neon blinks off and natural daylight is officially allowed back into town. This twice-daily electric convulsion is the only concession to the normal marks of time made by the casino owners, powers who forbid clocks or windows in their gambling rooms so that day and night pass by uncharted by anything more precise than vague degrees of desperation or euphoria, and time becomes something privately carried in the mind of each gambler, a quiet or needling companion creating its own idiosyncratic clock.

During my first night in Las Vegas, time had been subdued. It was now morning and I had not slept, had not even felt the slightest pull of drowsiness. Everything—my arrival, my baccarat victory, my memories, my golden whore—coexisted in a sharp, exhilarating present that refreshed itself over and over again. Everything in the room, from the artificially vermiculated furniture with ancien régime pretensions to my own abused but satisfied body, became joyful and vital presences that produced in me a feeling of pure incandescent being.

It seemed I had finally managed a weaving of thought and action that left no room in the soul's fabric for irony, parody, or any of the other over-civilized reflections that put restraints on exuberance. It mattered not at all that what I had won was no fortune, or that what I had tupped was an infantile whore: I felt I had, at the beginning of my voyage, gambled and won a moment for myself in which I could, if need be, live forever without complaint. And this allowed me to sit quietly through the Las Vegas sunrise and feel, with atavistic exultation, that everything it revealed complemented me.

Still, I made myself grow sober. I had, after all, promised that I would not be a mystic about gambling, that I would respect all of its formal intricacies. To win finally and decisively, of course, would mean a moment of uncalculated insight, a sudden *tolle et lude* at a craps or card table. But even the most ardent revelationist needs some form in which to put his intimations, some steps of humility whose order provides an outline for the spirit to follow.

I had chosen a rigid system of accounting as one of my disciplines, partly because I enjoyed setting down the equivalence in numbers of all the complex twists in a night of gambling, and partly because a plain record of arithmetical truths keeps one from rounding off wins and losses, from slipping into imagined sums that exist only in the conditional modes of recollection. I took out my notebook and carefully began doing my sums.

Initial viaticum
$17,480.00

Won	*Loss*
$3,000.00	0

Occupational expenses
a)	tips for dealers	$150.
b)	tips for waitresses	$ 4.
	Total:	$154.

Marginal estimated benefits
a)	free cigarettes	$ .50
b)	free drinks at baccarat table	$5.00
	Total:	$5.50

Miscellaneous expenses ordinary
a)	hotel	$35.
b)	taxi	$ 2.
	Total:	$37.

Miscellaneous expenses extraordinary
a)	one bottle Justerini & Brooks	$ 8.
b)	three bottles club soda	$ 1.
c)	one Oklahoma whore (bis)	$200.
	Total:	$209.

DEBITS	GROSS PROFITS
$400.	$3,005.50

NET PROFITS
$2,605.50

Setting down these numbers slowly, checking and recheck-ing their accuracy, made me feel limp and warm. Over and over again, I repeated the figures until they became an in-cantatory drone inside my head, a caressing swash of sound which I took to bed with me and which hummed me finally to sleep.

Tipur Sahib, the Tiger of Mysore, fat, swarthy, with a greased, popinjay's mustache, sits across the table from me. He has modernized himself: his suit is silk, blue, and double-breasted; his tie a polka-dot disease of red and gold; his tiny hands democratically denuded of all jewels except a large gold class ring from Harvard. Flanking him are enormous guards and vapid odalisques who bend over his shoulder as he sets out the cards between us. He says nothing, but I understand what the stakes are: his million against my left hand. A guard draws a long, gleaming scimitar from inside his coat and holds it a foot above the table, and I place the wagered part, palm downward, fingers splayed, upon the green velvet cover. The game is Five-Card Stud; the style, showdown. All cards are turned up, and whoever has the highest hand after ten are dealt wins. There is no sound as he begins with an ace for me and a ten for himself.

I look at Tipur Sahib, at his opaque brownness and ophidian eyes, at his smooth, pampered body which has experienced every pleasurable twitch a dark imagination could devise for it, and which has long ago stopped responding to any but the most exquisite sensual vibrations. I recognize him as the one who, a hundred years ago, gave the order to his English prisoners that they, with rough pieces of glass furnished for the task, amputate and swallow their prepuces. Then, of course, he had worn gold, pearls, and a fist-sized ruby in the center of a turban spiced at its crown with peacock feathers. His lips had been colored with a wine-red dye, and they had parted with a hint of agitated wonder as he watched the blood and banquet of foreskins from a throne of scented pillows. I had stood, a sliver of glass in my hand, waiting for years to be called before him until, hearing of my gambling, he decided to play poker for my body.

Tipur gives me a second ace and himself another ten, but he doesn't look at the cards. It seems that his eyes, while not blind, have grown tired of receiving the sights of the world. Nothing can light up the dark pupils, nothing can get through their thick ceramic glaze. From those eyes, my reflection comes back blankly at me, and I recognize how alone I am, how mad I have been to make this bet against someone so indifferent to striving, someone who knew all the corners of his fate at birth.

At this moment I know he has too great an advantage over me and, as two more cards are put down, I feel the beginning of a cry to stop, to call off the bet while I am still winning by the cards already dealt. But God I want his millions, and so two more cards fall in silence and I rise a bit now to wait for the last pair. I have two aces, a four and a seven; Tipur Sahib has two tens, a jack and a nine. Only eight cards can help him now, only eight out of forty-four left.

Forty-three after mine is delivered, a meaningless three of clubs. Tipur Sahib doesn't pause; his third ten comes down as silently and ugly as an erupting boil. I know what it means, but I try to hold back the knowledge. I look puzzledly at the ten red hearts as though their meaning were ambiguous, as though they were not an explicit end to the game we are playing.

Tipur, however, is not perplexed. He turns and rises gracefully from the table; and though I try, I cannot move my hand back from beneath the scimitar. *Again,* I cry. *Another hand! I'll bet another hand!* Tipur keeps rising and turning from the table, giving no indication from his padded shoulders that he has any interest in a second part of me. His women move in to watch the amputation. The air is now swollen with their erotic scent and there is a frenzied clacking of jewelry as bracelets and necklaces pendulate in the air. I can no longer see Tipur, but I must reach him and somehow force him to realize that I am still a diverting adversary.

With a tearing effort in my throat I shout: *My life! My life against another million!* And now there is silence. The ladies step back and a corridor is made for Tipur to return to the table. He does so with the air of someone who has forgotten a trifle. For an instant I am caught in his eyes, but my reflection is again flashed back undigested by Tipur's brain. He picks up the cards, deals an ace to himself and a jack of diamonds to me, and I know, from the way all promise and expectation flush out of my pores, that I am going to die when all the cards are dealt. I sink back into my chair, taking great gulps of the perfumed air. I breathe deeper and deeper until the sweetness puts a thick cover over my eyes and I slip away toward darkness cursing my fatal greed.

I came back to consciousness in Las Vegas screaming the same curses. Tipur! He has been grimly pursuing me since, at the age of ten, I read about his circumcision party. For a long time he disappeared, but once I began to gamble, at least twice a week he materialized for this game of poker, dressed like a Westerner but with the sealed brown mien of ancient Asiatic power. He always beat me in these dreams, but so far I had managed to wake up before he could collect even a finger of his winnings, and so we remained at a standoff. But to know that he was still there, in his wasp-waisted suit, waiting just beneath the level of my Las Vegas triumph, made me clearheaded and anxious. Several hours earlier I had felt free of all danger, as though last night's victory could never be stripped from me. As old and tired a dream as Tipur was, he was a chastening warning. I still had a long, vulnerable course to follow and there were hard work and spiritual maintenance to attend to.

First, then, to the bank. I had always enjoyed using these institutions as safe, respectable rest centers for my finances after a heavy campaign of gambling. With their loans, savings plans, Christmas clubs, stock counseling, credit services, and other categories of adult mercantile responsibility, they made me feel substantial whenever I used their strict but amiable world for my money. At the Las Vegas Bank of Commerce I stood, a patient, business-transacting citizen, in line at the window for traveler's checks. I was too much in transit to think of using one of their vaults, but I did want to convert $2,500 in cash into the more permanent appearance of property that bore my name.

In gambling, money goes through many stages of dress that affect its value. It can be no more substantial than a figure scribbled on a bookmaker's game sheet or a series of cabalistic sounds on a telephone wire; it can be a gaudy stack of pastel-colored chips—cash at a camp costume ball where its behavior will be frivolous and unpredictable; it can be as ragged and hopeless as a year-old marker patiently waiting in the folds of one's wallet and subsisting on dreams of redemption; it can have the genteel, indeterminate status of a delicately signed personal check; or, finally, it can be its essential self, slips of numbered paper bearing the heavy countenances of statesmen.

It is in this last condition that money is palpably the bones and arteries of a gambler. It is in this state, too, that money exudes a dangerous sense of fugaciousness, for one knows that there is nothing more into which it can evolve into, nothing of lesser consequence that it can pretend to be if suddenly dragged away to the opposite side of the table.

For this reason, during cool interludes, I like to see my

resources transferred into something that at least has a façade once or twice removed from hard cash. And so I bought twenty-five one-hundred-dollar traveler's checks, signed my name across each one carefully, and placed them in my hotel safety-deposit box where, left unmolested in the dark, they could ripen into a permanence that I would never attribute to dollars and cents.

It was one o'clock, the restaurants and snack bars were stuffed with sunburned, gabbling people, broken away from the pools and golf courses and planning over barbecued burgers which singer or spectacle they would take in that evening. I had not eaten for nearly twenty-four hours, so I ordered mounds of Western cooking and two Coca-Colas and settled into the happy, ravenous mood of those Sunday gamblers around me who had come to Las Vegas to play innocently, to lose the sums they had decided on at a vacation conference at home, and then, with perhaps a dollar chip as a souvenir, to depart unmarked by the world I had taken for my high seriousness.

One man I watched especially, a hulk of exuberance and thumping laughter. He wore a pale straw hat with miniature golf clubs tucked into its chartreuse band, salmon trousers, and a white mesh see-through sport shirt. He looked about fifty, but there was still a good store of strength in the chest he held in an arc and in the thick, knotty arms spread around two laughing women. He had six companions around him at the table, dressed in American tribal colors, friends and wives, all smiles with feigned gestures of exasperation as their leader hugged the ladies and, in a robust *Sprechstimme,* let loose a song rich in guileless obscenities. *Ah, ils sont dans le vrai?* Is it all that simple? Well, I thought, he might have a nightmare or two himself, and if he should meet his own Tipur, let us say to arm wrestle, he might, in his dark dream, see his white, muscled limb going down beneath Tipur's cocoa-hued pressure and hear the emasculating titter of the jeweled concubines.

He might have such a dream, and, if the egalitarian novelists are right, he might, too, know a despair so suffocating that a bullet somewhere beneath his green hatband would seem the only solution. But, as he sang on, I doubted this democratic ontology, not so much out of a wish for any general contentment in life as from a belief in an aristocracy of sensibility. One is born to the deeper agonies of existence the way one is born with patterned birthmarks or a Hapsburg chin, and if this expansive singer *should* blow his brains out, it would be because of some personal injustice, a terminal disease, an irremediable miscalculation in business. It would never be because of love or logic—the pure and noble reasons for self-annihilation.

And yet, he sang on, booming forth good times and affirmation. At least, I thought, if I ever come to sing to my family it will be a saga in bel canto, something elegant and boastful, something carefully wrought and decorated with well-modulated adventures. But scraping at the remains of my banana split, I admitted that I hadn't yet, after so many years, come upon a full, round voice for my aria; and, more, I had no one who wished to gather about hearths or restaurant tables to listen to me. This would always be the victory of the *vieux chapeau de golf;* for all my nobility and knowledge, he could still make me envy the healthy ambience of a middle-class meal.

"But," I thought, "you are not on your way around the world, ready to assault alien casinos, because you want to be loved. You've had the requisite mother, wife, child, lov-

93

ers, and have been dismal with them. Remember you have made an honest choice in taking this journey alone, so keep your pains in perspective. Or, even *be* excessive: brood over the Rhineland of a roulette table, become enamored of whorish angels, challenge and rechallenge the infidel Tipur until you are down to your last limb. But love? Love as family rhythms and household affection? Love in terms of compatible senses of humor and the slow transpiration of secrets? Love, then, in a Cape Cod beach house with a dungareed wife who, each summer, rereads Melville and works out her destiny ringed in by the sodden shorewear of your children?

"No, better to end alone in a furnished room with a demijohn of muscatel. And this is not a monstrous conclusion, for the love you want and may have to give depends on an effusion so intense that it is something that can be remembered or hoped for, but never lived with hour by hour. Accumulations, structures, comforts—everything that serves to build an edifice of affection only made you feel entombed. Now, with a day's gambling in front of you, don't begin to bemoan your solitude. You are more in the world at this moment than you have ever been before."

I paid and left the restaurant feeling that I had won an argument. I was tired of spiritual orphanage, tired of feeling that no matter how carefully I balanced my accounts, or how minutely I could examine the tissue of life, or how certain I was that in a Las Vegas restaurant only my mind was capable of encompassing itself and everything about it, I was not the presence, the fierce phenomenon that the singer a table away from me had been. I saw no longer any charm in being a poor Berkeleian object on which the whole world had turned its back and which has no vivacious eye of God to sustain it. I may have been alone, but I believed enough in the vitality of gambling so that weight, color, fever, extension, and all the other properties about which the imagination builds a persona, were self-evidently mine. I was going to begin gambling that day in a solid frame of mind, certain that I was a very substantial occupant of my particular space and time.

Chapter V

The voice bubbled behind me: "The score? What's the god-damned score?"

I twisted the swivel chair away from the television set and looked at the face suspended above me. Puffed, over-painted features burst in front of my eyes; long, blue-bordered teeth thrust toward me from receding gums; a rancid combination of alcohol and intestinal degeneration wafted over me. I froze as the face circled around me and became part of a round, twitching body that dropped into the chair next to mine. Surrounded by a nimbus of dyed red hair, the face spoke to me again: "The Giants ahead?"

"No score," I said, and then shivered a little.

"What inning?"

"Bottom of the third."

"I got the Giants for ten. They're a beautiful team, right? They're going to blow the Dodgers out of the park."

I barely nodded. A witch! A witch had flown into my calm

afternoon to announce she had bet the same team as I. A witch in cowboy boots, red, thigh-battling chinos, white blouse, and blue, bespangled range vest. Giant ruby-rimmed glasses swirled around her eyes, which were intently fixed on the tiny athletic images in front of her.

A witch, I thought. As chilling and ominous a witch as I have ever seen.

I was sitting in a large room lit partly by daylight, partly by a giant network of phosphorescent tubes that twisted across the ceiling and along the distant junctures of the walls. The effect was a sad, dusty glow that spread out sourly against the eyes like a polluted urban sunset. At the far end of the room, perhaps a hundred yards away, was a series of barred windows, behind which clerks transacted the establishment's business. Along the upper half of one wall ran a large blackboard, its milky-green surface broken up into hundreds of geometric compartments, each containing nominal abbreviations affixed to a set of numbers. Beneath this swirl of information stood a long dais, at which sat a second set of employees, their eyes protected from the sallow light by dark glasses or tinted visors. They scribbled, answered phones and, at intervals, proceeded up narrow metal ladders to change or add a number in the vast field of symbols suspended over them. The other people in the room, the establishment's customers, sat quietly on the huge leather divans and sofas, which, with flamboyant curves and angles, partitioned the vastness of the room into private enclosures. In that great space and etiolating light, faces lost any liveliness their features might have had, voices struck the ear like muted echoes, and the constant ring of the telephones produced a dull, subaqueous sound that had to it no tremor of emergency.

"I hate to miss the opening," the witch said. "I like watching the players all standing still with their hats off when they play 'The Star-Spangled Banner.' It really pumps up the excitement, and you get to see how many bald spots are on the team."

I nodded and turned a little away from her. She was definitely a bad omen, a vulgar sign. I should drift away as quickly as possible.

But there was something about the slow, impersonal rhythm of the building, like that of a Dickensian counting-house or a bus depot on a Sunday morning, that made it difficult to move at all. We were in the Hi-Life Sporting Club, an edifice that, tucked in among the phantasmas of the Las Vegas Strip, sits like a glum, functional rebuke to all the flamboyance and excess around it. However, what the Hi-Life actually houses is the largest bookmaking establishment in the country. Each day it handles hundreds of races; it establishes, through equally disinterested calculations, the odds on a political campaign or a college football game; it permits a gambler a passion about a golf match in Hawaii or a heavyweight fight in New York without the gambler's having to be, by nature, interested in or knowledgeable about the event. It is, finally, a colossal repository of contests that are continually being resolved, created anew, and wagered upon, and if it were in any other city in the country, the Hi-Life Sporting Club would be packed and rumbling with the action created by those compelled to risk something during the course of an ordinary day. However, being in Las Vegas, the Hi-Life's chief business is coldly conducted through the discipline of telephone orders, and those customers who come in person, who come to use the "club" facilities of leather sofas, television sets and sports magazines, are generally either the old who are in need of a place to rendezvous or the peculiar gamblers who prefer drawing out the tension of a single bet over the hours taken by a game of sport to squandering it in a few seconds of indulgence at a craps or blackjack table.

I had decided to start my day's gambling in such a place precisely because of its languid tempo. Later, during the night, when all the spirits of chance were loose in the city, I would have to risk the good feeling I'd acquired during my first day of traveling through the world. However, since last night I had won; since I was comfortable with myself and not oppressed by the loneliness of a traveler faced with an empty afternoon; since, in short, I felt I did not have to rush like a starveling to the tables, I had decided to pass the afternoon wrapped in one carefully selected sensation, one wager that would slowly reveal its consequences while I perpetuated my feeling of self-confidence.

In such a mood, I felt I should have had the outcome of an Austerlitz or Thermopylae to bet on. However, after checking the blackboard, I had found that the only contest left for the day was a baseball game between the Los Angeles Dodgers and the San Francisco Giants, with the Dodgers listed as 7-to-5 favorites. I scaled down my desire for diversions and bet five hundred dollars on the Giants.

There was a wheeze of invective next to me as a Giant batter ended the inning by striking out. The witch began digging furiously in a large straw shopping bag, from which she snatched a rose-colored inhaler and plunged it deeply into each nostril.

"It gets to my sinuses when I gamble. They fill up like ditches in a rainstorm."

I winced. I was now certain that I was going to be the victim of a spell, that the spectacled sorceress was going to cost me my detached self-confidence, as well as my five hundred dollars.

I should perhaps explain that all sensitive gamblers have

known witches and believed in their powers to varying degrees. These ladies materialize generally when one's concentration is at its fiercest and always when one is deep within a winning rhythm. In an instant, they are simply there, and they manage to emanate a subtle psychic disturbance that draws the mind away from the gamble at hand and forces it to fix itself on their presence. Will-lessly, one slowly looks up from the table and confronts a face without human aspect, a face that is old without having been honestly aged, and whose features reveal a bitter moribundity.

Invariably, if one is betting hundreds, the witch pointedly risks only a dollar or two, just enough so that her power will, penetrate into the game. And the attuned gambler knows at once that this power has him as its object, that her dollar is conjoined to his hundreds in some dark way, and that until he can recapture his own ego, his fate is going to be directed by an unpitying crone who will manipulate it at her pleasure.

Of course, not all gamblers consider witches pernicious. There are some who actually are relieved to find themselves held in thrall by one of them, who happily give up their personal whims and follow her calculations and choices at the table. And sometimes they manage to win a little by doing so. But most players, and I include myself in this group, know that witches are there to mock them, to present a travesty of desire and aspiration, to bespeak a tawdry end to all human risk.

However, the more I glimpsed of the specimen next to me, the more she seemed an odd example of her kind. There was definitely an essence of witchness about her, but it was diffused with an apparent genuine excitement that gave her face a look of ardor and concern whenever something of interest happened on the screen in front of us. Like her sisters, she had invaded and discomfited my mind, but she had done it openly, crashing into my afternoon with raucous intimacy rather than compelling coldness. There was even something comic about her as she sat muttering epithets and encouragement, and I felt that beneath the cata-strophic makeup there might actually be touchingly human lineaments.

"Why the hell can't they hit this sonofabitch?" she said to me after again going to the shopping bag and bringing out some Kleenex squares with which she relieved her ex-citable sinuses.

"A tough pitcher," I answered. "Shut the Giants out the last time he faced them. You can get a record sheet at one of the windows."

She looked startled that I had actually spoken. Her eyes, behind the baroque glasses, took a scan of me and then shot back to the television screen.

"All he's got is that fast ball," she said loudly. "Fast ball, fast ball, fast ball. Our Giants should get it timed and then explode. He's a good-looking, sassy bastard, though. Look at the way he kicks up in the air when he throws."

Yes, I was beginning to think that she was not a witch, that my instinctive uneasiness over her appearance must have been caused by her carnal absurdity rather than by any spiritual menace she carried with her. Indeed, I began to feel that she was someone almost excessively human, a great daubed clown of a person who sported wild, overripe breasts rather than withered dugs. The more she enthused over the happenings in front of her, the more vulnerable she appeared, as if something of greater moment were attached to the outcome of the game than the loss of her ten dollars.

Whatever she was, she was out of place in the Augustan order of my afternoon. I made up my mind to move, to give her a courteous "good luck" and find another television set. However, before I could make the beginnings of an excusable exit, the Giants put on a little rally—a walk, two singles, and a double—and the gamester's tenet of not abandoning a winning seat took precedence over the unsettling nature of my neighbor.

During our team's flurry, the woman had sniffed and squealed with approval. Mixed with the usual fan's encouragements, however, were her admiring estimates of the men's physiques. The player who doubled, for example, received a breathy approbation, and the following batter, who popped out ignominiously, nevertheless won praise for broad shoulders and rugged forearms. In fact, as the game progressed, hardly a player passed into view who did not have his attributes commented on in a pungent manner.

"Best-looking men in the world, baseball players," she said between innings. "Where else can you find bodies like that? Of course, now and then you get an old relief pitcher that's running a bit to fat, but most of the time you'd be hard put, sweetheart, to find a better collection of American men than what steps out on a baseball field."

A baseball fetishist, I thought. Not a witch at all. Only a compulsive admirer of men in caps and knickers.

"Football players," she went on, seeing that she had caught my attention, "are just a little too damned much. They've got what you could call bodies of the future, which is fine for those who are going to *live* in the future. But, honey, baseball players are the right size for a woman who definitely won't make it out of this century."

She laughed nervously when she finished making this distinction, as if she had caught herself being emphatic in the presence of a stranger about a personal whim. She sat quietly until the Dodgers were retired in order in the top of the fifth inning, and then, for the first time in a soft voice, asked me if I were a baseball fan.

"Not really," I said.

"Then you're a bettor," she said sadly. "Look, I know I can be annoying. I mean I get excitable over things and sometimes—well, I don't want to upset you or anything if you've got a bundle on the game."

Her saying this made me feel a throb of shame over the uncharitable thoughts I'd had about her.

"You've got money on the game, too," I said.

"Yeah, but only enough to get my sinuses clogged up and to give me the right to use these *luxurious* facilities."

She glanced bitterly toward the dais as she spoke, and I imagined that her appearance and behavior had, in the past, occasioned rebukes and threats of banishment from several of the clerks who labored there.

"I only come here," she went on, "because, even though it's a goddamned tomb of a place, it's better than sitting in my glorious Sunrise Motel apartment surrounded by old Colt 45 cans and Kleenex. I mean you shouldn't watch a baseball game alone, and it's nice to put a little bit on the game to get the juices flowing. I've lived in this town for six years; I know something about gambling. But my real kick comes from looking at the players. I mean it's beautiful to see good-looking men nowadays doing something really American."

She paused for a moment to hiss an obscenity as a Dodger batter singled, and then, perhaps catching a little twitch in my expression when the player stole second on the first pitch, resumed an apologetic manner toward me.

"As I was saying, if you're in deep on this game, I'll get me another seat."

I insisted that she stay, partly because I was too proud to admit that anything could nettle me, partly because the Dodger base runner had been thrown out at the plate in an attempt to score on a sharp single to left, and partly because I was angry with myself for having been so squeamish. I had come out into the world to gamble, and there was no place in whatever journey I would finally make for an irrational aversion to a woman with whom I actually had something in common. At the very least we formed an alliance against the dim scriveners watching us from the dais.

"Your sitting next to me in Las Vegas isn't going to affect what happens in San Francisco," I said, not at all certain that this was really so. I had been sunk in superstition since the lady arrived, and it was not easy to slip back, without misgivings, into enlightenment.

My companion sensed that my explanation was too pat.

"Yeah, that makes sense, but gamblers don't often look at it that way. If you walk around this town and try to have fun, it seems you're always in somebody's way. Hell, I know I look a little strange, but this is as good as I can put it together, honey. If I was real tasteful about myself, you know what I'd look like? A nice gray-haired old lady who's out of the game for good."

I stared at her and tried to imagine what game she was still in. I could see her slouched in the corner of a dark cocktail lounge, perhaps, coming to some romantic understanding with an aging, sun-wrinkled cowboy in for a night on the town. I could see them both stagger off to her motel apartment, where she would nervously perform a moment's housekeeping. I could watch her abandon the attempt and defiantly kick the afternoon's Colt 45 cans around the room, while her companion roared with something like laughter and opened the bottle they had brought with them from the bar. I could follow them as they stumbled toward an unmade bed surrounded by full ashtrays, dirty glasses, and pills that had been prescribed for a dilapidated nervous system. I could even hold them in focus until, after a liquor-spilling embrace, they fell among the wrinkled linen and huddled together to begin a half-conscious coupling.

And that is as far as my imagination could take them. It would need a saintly mind to sustain the concluding details of such a vision, and a saint would naturally follow the principle of universal humanity and think, "Well, I am part of what they do. It is I, too, who am in that pathetically mortal embrace on a rumpled motel bed."

But then a saint has consolations that I did not have at that moment, and though we had bet the same side of a baseball game, I wasn't going to admit that there were deep similarities between me and those who are made ragged by life.

"Anyway"—my companion was still explaining her presence—"I've given up worrying about who I spook in this town. There's too many crazy and just plain mean men in Las Vegas to worry over them. I like baseball, I like a little bet, I want company and I don't want to spend the afternoon in a bar, 'cause I've got no self-control and I'd be pissed by the ninth inning. So like it or not, Betsy's right here."

Her expression had just enough of a challenge to it so that I knew she was offering me one last chance to leave. Instead, I introduced myself and we settled back to watch our team take a three-run lead into the sixth inning.

"Have you ever been to a bullfight?" Betsy asked as a Dodger batter began a perfunctory protest of a called third strike. I answered that I had and that I enjoyed them.

"I thought I would, too," she said testily. "A girlfriend of mine and I once went down to Tijuana just to see some bullfights—or to be honest, some bullfighters. All my life I'd heard about how damned beautiful they looked in their little suits and slippers, with their asses wrapped in satin. Well, I saw a few and they were a mean disappointment."

"Most of them," I said, thinking back on dozens of melo-dramatic Spanish Sundays *a las cinco de la tarde*, "look a little morose and undernourished."

"Sad and scrawny is what you mean," Betsy laughed. "I mean the only thing they have going for them is the fact that they can get a horn through their privates at any moment, and that makes a woman feel, well, a little sympathetic. But I could never take them seriously as someone you'd want to bed down with. Now baseball players, their asses are just as appealing, to my way of thinking, as the bullfighters', and you get a whole solid man along with it."

Betsy looked approvingly at the television images and gave them a quick hand-to-forehead salute.

"And then," she said sharply, "there's death. My girlfriend kept going on about how bullfighters are always close to death, like that's some big deal. An eighty-year-old man is close to death, but no one wants to shack up with him because of it."

I was a little abashed at this logic. I had always felt, to be sure, that certain poets had injudiciously conjoined copulation and death; but I, too, had often used mortality as a special argument for making love, and I did not like to see this honorable, romantic plea fall prey to the *reductio ad absurdum* of an octogenarian's body. It was a point, however, that I didn't want to debate with Betsy while the game was in progress. Instead, feeling that she wanted some barroom intimacy from me, I asked her if she had ever actually made love to a baseball player. It was apparently the right question. She seemed to relax for the first time since her arrival while she considered a reply. Smiling, she ran her tongue across her lips and began to rock slowly toward an affirmative answer.

"My first husband was a utility infielder with the Giants."

"The New York Giants?"

"Well, with their organization. He was heading for the majors as soon as he learned to hit a curve ball a little better. But then the war came along and he was taken off and killed in New Guinea. He was twenty years old, wiry, but with big bones. And there were two things he took serious —me and the game we're watching. But then I guess he took the war serious, too, because he enlisted right away and they sent me a Silver Star for what he did to get himself killed."

She paused for a moment, looked hard at the television set, and then shuddered a conclusion.

"You know, I'd take them all on. Every guy on every team in the major leagues, black or white, batting-practice pitchers or twenty-game winners. They're the best damn men in the country, and playing our country's game, too. Hell, taking them on would be like taking on America. What woman, who's gone through two husbands and a lot of side action, and who lost a damned good-looking infielder in a foreign war, wouldn't want to do that?"

A sexual jingoist. An erotic patriot. What she had told me might well have been the dreams of a lonely woman, but it sounded more like the affirmation of a fellow citizen who was getting far more pleasure from the state's dispensations than I was.

I looked at Betsy, whose eyes were now tearing a bit, and I thought about baseball, about her infielder's war, and about someone who had wanted me to love America at an early age and how I had disappointed him.

It was late in the summer of 1944, and the cause of democratic freedom was inexorably beating down the evil yellow men of the Pacific jungles and the sadistic blond beasts who, in Europe, did their Führer's will. It was a time when the imaginations of all my friends were filled with the notion of dying well, and one could not walk very far through the desolate lots of Jackson Heights without seeing boys going through the stylized rituals of battlefield death as learned from the films that had invented them. Through fenced-in fields we stalked enemy emplacements; suddenly a burst of falsetto machine-gun fire counterpointed against a basso of grenade explosions. Those struck by the former were expected to pirouette at least once before hitting the ground, while those meant to simulate bodies torn by shell fragments could improvise any sort of leap they pleased, as long as it was executed with flailing limbs and no attempt was made to cushion the fall and spoil the realism of the moment. After the initial ambush came the specialty at which I excelled: the ultimate survivor from the slaughtered squad who, enraged over the fate of his comrades, charges blindly toward the enemy and is felled by a single sniper's bullet. The art to this enactment was to plop immediately to the ground with no embellishments whatever, and thus testify to the deadly anatomical accuracy of the unseen marksman. After this brief coda, the lot would be strewn with unmoving bodies while, for several minutes, each of us lay in a frozen attitude and, as boys burdened by our futures, enjoyed the wonderful lack of responsibility that seemed to come with dying well.

Except for these mock battles, and their pleasant sense of annihilation, the only other vivid image I had of how the adult world made war was obtained from the storefront of an empty building which I passed once a week on my way to shop at a special bakery my mother favored. Since the store was always deserted, I never knew whether an organization or an individual was responsible for the gruesome placards mounted behind an unwashed window that bore no commercial or political markings. Whoever placed those pictures there, however, knew how to impress upon a young imagination the way war turns the world upside down and lets loose all sorts of personal terrors.

The placards changed each time I passed, but their theme was constant: the perpetration by Nazis of bodily humiliations. One, I remember, showed a group of women—some already naked, some in the process of disrobing—standing despairingly before a row of cages they were about to enter, while S.S. officers, whips in hand, leered and laughed at their degradation. Another depicted the mutilation of an American flier: stripped to the waist, on his knees, his flight cap still worn at a jaunty angle, he stared defiantly at his jackbooted tormentors who were in the process of amputating his arms with long, curved, tasseled swords.

These threats to the form and dignity of the body, rather than any implied danger to the democratic freedoms that were taught to me at school, always made me dash home to be reassured by my mother that America was really winning the war. I could tolerate dying, or what I imagined dying to be from those minutes of post-battle stillness in our neighborhood fields; but to stand naked before those inhuman expressions, or to have the completeness of my body destroyed—these fates made me pray every night for the obliteration of my country's enemies, and at the same time to yearn darkly for such totalitarian powers as the storefront pictures had shown me.

If my desire for victory was based on personal fear, my mother's was occasioned by esthetic annoyance. To her, the war was a vulgar interruption of what she called the flow of civilization, a moment of madness that had, of course, some excitement to it, but that was, in the end, a gross enterprise. She believed in a world of adventure and personal combat, but this was only for a select few. There was no audacious style to a war in which millions wore untailored uniforms and slaughtered for political principles, and the only battle toys she bought me were expensively modeled replicas of fighter planes with a single seat in the cockpit.

My father, however, was aglow with patriotism at this time. In the spring of 1944, he returned from a year's tour with a U.S.O. show that had moved from camp to camp in the Far West and then ended in the Aleutian Islands. With him he brought some curiosities from the war—a Japanese flag, a dozen machine-gun bullets, shoulder patches from each division he had entertained, and an accordion on which the wounded he'd played for had scratched their names.

Until that spring, I remember my father as one who moved cautiously around the edges of my life, bringing, every Sunday, a divorced parent's diffidence into my world and a sense of what it was like to make a cautious covenant with life, a compact in which the extraordinary had been bargained away in exchange for simple survival. Even when he played the piano, he never improvised, never went further than a grace note beyond the standard melodies of the popular tunes he lived on as a singer's accompanist and cocktail pianist. He had once, my mother told me, while first touring with jazz bands through the South, been willing to display his musical imagination for a chorus or two, but this improvisational spirit died bit by bit as he encountered musicians who could sing, harmonize, and turn phrases through their instruments with an articulateness he could never match. He decided to play nothing but the notes he saw before him, and he gave his entire life up to similar imperatives and a belief that a vague universal justice would reward those who did their best to add only the most traditional pains and pleasures to the world.

But that spring my father came as close to being ecstatic

as I ever remember him. He was swollen with the moral excellence of his country and with the military victory it was already beginning to digest. He was in love with the image of the American warrior. He told me jagged, emotional tales about the pluck and courage of the wounded he had played for, of how multiple amputees would sing along with his standard version of "Don't Sit Under the Apple Tree," and how the paralyzed sparkled when the troupe's female singer kissed and whispered them their country's gratitude. During the last months of the war, he was intoxicated with patriotism and certain that the dialectic of history had finally resolved itself into a Christian-American destiny.

"You know, old pal," he would say to me, "when you see what this country is really about, you understand how everything fits. I mean how else could we have pulled a wilderness together and made it a place that the rest of the world envies so much that they would crawl on their knees to squeeze in here among us. But we don't want people on their knees—except when they're praying. No, we want tall, straight, wonderful guys, guys you'd be proud to die with, guys who'll never be pushed around because they know what their history is. Never forget it, you're living in a country of glory."

Thus spake Arthur Richardson, five-feet-two-inches tall, to his son who only understood the need, at all costs, to avoid mutilation and personal shame. We were destined for conflict long before history failed to carry out his prophecies and he became convinced that an unholy subversion had taken place. During the Fifties, he wrote letters to the *Daily News*, encouragement to the F.B.I., and anti-Communist songs ("I'll Never Be a Slave or Love a Tractor," etc.). He dreamed of bombs, great purifying explosions that would obliterate forever the flat profiles and shadowy pigments of those who, with alien arrogance, had clotted the flow of American virtue throughout the world. Alone, in a basement apartment, he struggled to maintain the respect he had felt for himself when it seemed that his country had been bequeathed a magnificent, self-evident destiny. When I would visit him and prod his arguments with my facile student's logic, he would, in furious rejoinder, bring out his autographed accordion and answer me with the songs he had played for the wounded of World War II. Even in a rage, his blazing eyes fixed on me, he never changed or colored a note. Still, the passion with which he played in order to shore up his besieged visions made "I'll Be Seeing You" and "When Johnny Comes Marching Home" shimmer with a demonism that would astonish me into silence. In that subterranean room, with linoleum on the floor and pictures of Washington, Eisenhower, and myself as a child on the wall, my father was gradually sinking into the static, galling madness of the citizen who had put his trust in the state and hoped thereby to gain some special splendor to his life. Nevertheless, it was only in those moments of ludicrous fury that I remember him sounding like a true musician, who, if he could not make music beautiful, could make it terrifying.

But in 1944 my father beamed with health and optimism, and when he sensed that the national wartime spirit was absent from his son's world, he announced that I was to see my first professional baseball game. It would be an event, he impressed upon me, that would display the essence of American virtue. As one among equals, I would be able to cheer or deride the efforts of my team as I saw fit. I could howl curses at authority whenever I disagreed with the umpires and thousands would augment the sounds of my displeasure because, as fellow fans, they would share and understand my feelings. In short, my father was anxious to teach me what it was like, in America, to join a crowd.

For a time, at the Polo Grounds, I was indeed overwhelmed by the first real spectacle I had ever seen. From my father next to me to the tiniest human blotch at the opposite end of the stadium, I felt a flow of connecting energy. I had, after all, never before been among such a number of people, never seen thousands and thousands of strangers rising in ordered rows around me, settling into a single purpose.

And then, there were the colors of Coogan's Bluff: the chromatics of the slim, triangular pennants atop the stadium roof; the luxuriant emerald of the outfield; the decisive whiteness of the baselines; the blunt, sepia-toned advertisements along the walls and buildings on the hillside; the flamboyance of professional baseball uniforms; and, finally, the sweeping pointillism of sport shirts and faces that shimmered into a pastel haze whenever the eye relaxed.

I was unquestionably dazzled, and my father beamed and coaxed me into deeper enthusiasm with the exotic food and drink of the ball park. We joked, feasted, and, whenever a soldier came into view, my father explained to me the significance of the ribbons he wore and how his heroism had made our afternoon possible.

And then "The Star-Spangled Banner" was played. My father rose, took my hand, and, with the other, placed his straw hat above his heart. He began to sing, as did others around us; the soldiers in the stands saluted; the players bared their heads and faced their country's flag blowing above the roof in center field. Happy unity and concord were everywhere: the war coming triumphantly to an end; the national game about to be played; glorious, cloudless Sunday skies. As my father pressured my hand, I, too,

113

joined in on the last chorus of our national anthem, struggling, as I did each morning at school, with the elusive melody.

But I went no further. Just before the game began, I started to draw back from the feeling of community my father was offering me. Suddenly, I began to feel threatened by so much collective life, as though it might all turn on me if it sensed that I was watching and judging it. Still, though frightened, I found myself refusing to surrender my ego to the common zeal around me. The self I was secretly putting together as a child was now making its first exclusive demands, and no matter what virtue lay at the heart of a democratic gathering, it was not going to be part of anything so undistinguished as a throng's enthusiasm.

As the game went on, I wrapped myself securely in my own perceptions. Soon, as though I wanted to challenge the general goodness that my father had urged me to discover in the ball park, I began making brutal improvisations on the phenomena in front of me. By the fifth inning or so, I was imagining each ballplayer who struck out being dragged to center field where, after a signal from me, he was ceremoniously beheaded. And by the game's end, after a slow escalation of such indignities, I had turned the ball park into a Flemish hell; the banners into flapping gargoyles; the players into wild, defecating beasts; the stadium into a giant caldron in which everyone, save myself, writhed, howled, and bubbled into vapor.

It was the first time that I had ever turned my imagination against the world, and I was pleasantly amazed to find that I could have such sport with adult reality without suffering immediate retribution. Of course, I did not know then that I had done nothing more than take the first step toward confinement in the mental oubliette in which I would live for years with the richest moments of my existence stretched out upon the rack of a prim estheticism. As my father and I left the stadium in strained silence that afternoon, I only knew, with some relief, that I would never have to grow up to be like those whose names had decorated his accordion.

That night, lying in bed, I heard my father speaking in the next room.

"He never cheered," he was saying in a hollow voice. "He just sat and watched, and never cheered once at anything."

I remember that phrase turning over in my mind as I went to sleep, smugly certain that no one would ever know what I really felt, who I really was.

"Jesus Christ!" Betsy snorted and sent a wadded Kleenex bouncing off the television screen. It was not an excessive gesture. Only three outs away from a victory, the descendants of the team my father had taken me to see were beginning to falter. A triple had scored the leadoff batter who had walked, and the relief pitcher who had been summoned proved unable to throw accurately. Four straight balls, and the Dodgers now had runners on first and third and there was no one out.

Had I been duped by feigned human appetites and American pride? Was Betsy really a citizen of nothing but negation after all?

She must have caught the accusing look in my eyes. Her face ducked behind a cluster of tissues that she held in her hand, and she twisted her cowboy boots into a contrite, pigeon-toed position.

"We'll get out of the game all right, sweetheart," she whined. "We're just getting a little extra thrill for our money, that's all."

After coming so far through the afternoon without problems, the sudden prospect of having to accept a loss was an especially painful shock. I had already mentally added the seven hundred dollars to my total wealth, so that now I could only be diminished by the game's conclusion, and while I sat nonchalantly slouched in my chair, I raged at myself for having let my concentration on the present gamble dissolve into fuzzy speculation and for having, like a glory-swollen general, forgotten the possibility of peripeteia.

"I've known a lot of men like this sonofabitch of a pitcher," Betsy wailed as, after a second successive base on balls, the Dodgers loaded the bases. "Look at him! No juice. Couldn't be more than twenty-three years old, and no goddamned juice."

As well as cursing myself, I cursed Betsy's shrill voice, which had caused several pale employees' heads to be turned our way. If we were going to lose, I wanted to do it without setting up a general squall that would make everyone privy to our troubles.

"Come on, honey," Betsy said, moving her chair closer to mine. "Let's root this kid home." Then she touched my arm lightly and added: "I swear I haven't jinxed this game for you."

I was beyond caring now about the likelihood of Betsy's being preternatural. The whole afternoon was sinking around me, and I felt the most important thing left for me to do was to be calmly lucid in the face of possible disaster. The lessons of past gambling had taught me to train my mind so that it never assumed a loss before it actually occurred; but, at the same time, I wanted to be prepared for a setback in my Las Vegas fortunes, and to feel, with minute exactness, the details of its effects. I did not want to be dumbly overwhelmed.

Betsy, on the other hand, was fighting with undignified fierceness for her ten dollars. She was straddling the arm of her chair as though it were a skittish charger, and her voice was now of such a pitch that even the deadening acoustics of the Hi-Life Club could not subdue it.

"C'mon, you sorry bastard, stop dragging your ass on the ground." Her finger, reaching out and sharply tapping the television screen, indicated the young pitcher as her subject of abuse. "You got more heart than that. Stop hanging your goddamned head and remember you're major league, baby, major league!"

The pitcher, who had been petulantly kicking up little explosions of dirt around the mound, finally took a deep breath and squared himself away to face his opponent. He wound up and threw his first strike of the afternoon.

"That's better," Betsy shrieked, and when his next pitch was fouled off, she went on: "We'll make it yet, sonny. If we can just keep goosing you along, we're all going to have a good day."

The next two pitches were spirit-dampening balls, and Betsy anxiously took hold of my hand. Hers was bony and damp, but I made no attempt to slip out of its grasp. I held on docilely as she swiveled in her chair, feeling a little ashamed of the comfort her gnarled fingers were giving me.

Be careful, I told myself. Just watch and try to want nothing. Don't root like an undershirted fan in the last row of the bleachers. Those who are indifferent are those who are rewarded.

A third strike, and an ululation erupted from Betsy. It rang through the tired air of the building and caused clerks to pull their visors down in a huff and angrily snap pencils in two. It also drowned out a small, delighted howl that I had belched out involuntarily.

"You know what we need now, don't you?" Betsy laughed, shaking her inhaler at me. It was coated with her dried secretions, but I forced myself not to avert my eyes. "You know what we need now to take a little money out of this morgue!"

Her face was now complete chaos. Rouge, powder, lipstick, mascara had oozed into macabre blendings. Her eyes were red and wet; her nose overflowed.

"Are you lucky?" she said in an urgent whisper to me.

"I'm trying to find that out," I answered.

"Well I'm not. But you know, if I work my ass off, I can always seem to do just a little bit better than break even. So do you know what I think I'll do to show my faith in this kid? I'm going to hold my breath till he walks off the mound a winner."

With that, she took a great gulp of air, swelled out a bit, and fixed her protruding eyes on our pitcher.

If she dies, I thought, from a stroke or from slow suffocation through a Dodger rally, I will be a long time disengaging her hand. I'll be forced to drag after her body to wherever it is in Las Vegas they take the recently dead. And it will be, since no one will claim kinship or amity with her, I who take final custody of her boots and shopping bag. Well, if it means being a fool to end the afternoon happily, then I'll don a belled cap and pantaloons. There are many paths for a righteous gambler to take.

It was a relief to slough off dignity. I filled my lungs with an enormous intake of air and sealed my lips tightly. Betsy felt this little convulsion of my body and gave me a welcoming wink. One pitch later, as we both began to tremble from lack of oxygen, the Dodger batter lined into a game-ending double play and we had won.

We gasped and gulped for air, and then we cheered the Giants and each other. Betsy spun jubilantly in her chair, and I, still fastened to her hand, skipped a circle around her like a joyful satellite. When I felt her gravity draw me toward her, I opened my arms so that we could embrace and twirl together.

Our moment in orbit was stopped by a huge, hirsute hand belonging to one of the Hi-Life's managers. He looked at Betsy with belittling tolerance and at me with outright contempt.

"Don't break up the furniture just because you won a few bucks," he said quietly, and then turned his back on us and walked away as if there were no possibility that we might protest his ending our celebration so abruptly.

He was right. Chastened, we rose, smoothed ourselves out, and looked shyly at each other.

"We'll celebrate someplace else," I said.

Betsy nodded, and, with hand mirror and compact, went to work putting her face back into the little order it had had when she arrived.

"You thought when I sat down that I was going to ruin your luck, didn't you?" she asked, looking hard into the small mirror.

"I'm a superstitious snob," I said.

"That's all right," she said, tossing the compact with a sharp click of exasperation back into the bag. "You got a right to be a snob. It's a free country." Then, loud enough so that the manager would hear her: "It's a free country everywhere in America except in this goddamned funeral parlor."

She got up and looked straight at me. "Okay, let's pick up our money and go have a few drinks someplace."

She was daring me to make an excuse, but I had no intention of doing so. I just wondered, as she went off to the ten-dollar clerk and I to the one who handled hundred-dollar bettors, how much of an obligation I had incurred.

It was a low suspicion. When I was through being paid,

I looked about and found that Betsy had vanished. I started to leave the club to find her, but thought better of it. We had formed a happy, raucous crowd together, and I felt freer for having been a part of it. But crowds must finally dissolve back into individuals, each of whom has secrets and a separate way to go home.

Chapter VI

There were two rows of strangers ringed around me, and their eyes beamed adulation. From behind the velvet rope that separated the baccarat table from the rest of the casino, they watched and murmured, keyed to my slightest movement. In front of me were my tokens of specialness: two stacks of hundred-dollar bills, one representing the seven hundred dollars I had brought with me to the table, the other the two thousand or so I had won since sitting there. A serving-girl, silver tray in hand, who had appeared after my first thousand-dollar bet, was my personal attendant. When not occupied by my requests for brandy, she stood a few steps back from my chair, at almost military attention in her uniform of pink leotard, black boots, and green net stockings decorated with flesh-revealing rips along her inner thighs. I resolved to ask that fresh stockings be put on when I had won five thousand.

On my left sat my beaming squire. He was neatly dressed in a servile gray suit, white shirt, and blue, symmetrically winged bow tie. His round, fiftyish face wore a hectic glow, and he sighed Midwestern expressions of wonder and fealty whenever I won a bet of several hundred dollars and he, in imitation commensurate with his rank, added twenty-five dollars to his total worth. He had been, so he told me, a drab loser, buffeted by the furies that torment the lower orders of Las Vegas bettors, until I had sat next to him. A salesman who had stolen a few days from his commercial itinerary in order to sport and lust awhile in Las Vegas, he had discovered that, alone, he was susceptible to ruin.

"I was the slow hog in the slaughterhouse," he told me after confessing that he'd stayed five days and fifteen hundred dollars past the allotment he'd allowed himself for a salesman's caprice. Nevertheless, though toying with catastrophe, he had remained neat and in good humor. I was therefore pleased to admit him to my evening's train.

On my right, an empty seat between us, sat an enchanting shill. A dark, fully blossomed woman, she indifferently handled the cards and money in front of her, accepting a functionary's role while maintaining the appearance of one who has known better days and bigger gambles. Her assignment from the casino management had obviously been to divert me, to fill in the dead moments of play with chatter and seduction so that I wouldn't be tempted to take my winnings to another establishment's tables. She had tried a few bits of amiable badinage on me earlier in the evening— bland comments on my luck and uninspired inquiries into my reasons for being in Las Vegas—but I hadn't let her dilute my concentration on, and commitment to, the evening's cards. I was polite in my responses, but I let her understand that I knew whose bidding she did and that, so long as we remained at the baccarat table, she was not going to clutter my mind with erotic images of prerevolutionary Havana.

Facing me across the length of the table was a figure who I had felt instantly was my adversary. He was large, thickly built, with hair that looked as if it had been arranged strand by strand. He was well-manicured, well-scrubbed, and the suit he wore of celadon flannel clung without wrinkles to the outlines of his body. With a round face that had been shaved and patted into blandness, my opponent glowed like a polished semiprecious stone. He obviously considered himself a perfectly finished human item, and managed his dress and toilet accordingly. This was enough for me, a fresh disciple of flux and conation, to issue him a silent challenge.

One seat away from me, separated by the salesman, was the lady of the table. For the half-hour that she had been playing, her face had remained fixed in a pacific smile, her attitude interested in the proceedings but indifferent to the fate of the small bets she placed for herself. She looked at us, the other players, as if we were strange, delightful beings whose kind she had never seen before. She was a woman who, because she had lived for a while with her beauty, seemed no longer concerned about its maintenance, so that, compared to the meticulous dress and coiffures of the other ladies in the casino, hers was pleasantly casual. She looked ripened and amused by life—a woman before whom a man must act with some courage and no self-importance.

The game went on, and I continued to win. For every bet I lost, I won at least two, and there had not been a single reversal whenever I felt the urge to escalate the sums. I pushed further and further on with my units of wager, and by the time the third shoe of the evening had been exhausted, I had reached the table's limit of two thousand.

While the dealers gathered the dead cards together and began the elaborate ritual of shuffling, I counted the stack of money in front of me. It came to slightly less than five thousand dollars and formed a mound of hundred-dollar bills high enough to cause brief exclamations of awe from the salesman.

"That's a half-year's commission you've got stacked in front of you."

I nodded, outwardly indifferent, and began recounting the stack of money.

"If I could play this game like you, I'd rent the chair I'm sitting in for the year."

I separated the twenties and tens from the pile, and then began placing the hundreds in stacks of ten in front of me.

"I'm not lying. I wouldn't need a house, car, a job or a friend. This chair would be my only possession."

I was now beginning my third count. The lady of the table was looking at me, her smile an approbation, her eyes insinuating nothing but joy over my good feeling. The Cuban shill was moody, and could do no more than hiss a compliment or two about my good fortune. My opponent in the green flannel suit, who, since I had purposely wagered against his choices, was losing perhaps as much as I had won, had allowed a strand or two of hair to become unfixed and drop across his tanned, greaseless forehead.

"You know," my loyal Midwesterner went on, "I'm almost even now. I never thought I'd see daylight again, and, thanks to you, it's almost high noon."

I smiled at him and ordered the torn-stockinged serving-girl to bring us a pair of brandies. For a moment, I tipped my chair back an inch or two and let all the rays of envy and admiration coming from the game's audience focus on the spoils I'd taken. Then, since the dealers were still not ready for another shoe, I began counting again.

I confess that the joy this tallying gave me was of no higher order than that of the miser who confirms, with base arithmetic, his worldly success. But, to be fair, perhaps those wizened figures of fairy tales and Victorian novels, so sorely mocked because they would not spend their wealth on ordinary tokens of happiness, simply could not tolerate the notion of limited existence. Instead, they put their faith in an eternity of addition, in a life that could be perpetuated forever if cached-away piles of silver were made inexorably to increase with each counting.

Whatever the cause, the counting gave me satisfaction. I had set a ten-thousand-dollar goal for myself when I came to Las Vegas and, in slightly more than twenty-four hours, even reckoning hard expenses and casual pleasures, I was now within seven hundred dollars of my objective. One more winning play and I could move on, a victor in my first trial.

The dealers finally finished with the cards, and a full shoe was placed in front of me. In case that I'd miscalculated what was needed to reach the ten-thousand-dollar limit, I bet a thousand. The salesman remained faithful to my fortune and wagered a hundred. *La Cubana* made a perfunctory minimum bet, as did the smiling lady. Pointedly, but in a well-mannered way, my adversary bet a sum equal to my wager against me. The croupier called for cards, and I dealt a pair to myself and the same to my immaculate opponent.

He turned over a natural eight, I revealed two kings, a losing hand, a baccarat. For a moment I felt, deep in my stomach, a twitch of fear, a visceral warning that the evening's luck would change if I pressed on. However, for twenty-four hours I had subjected myself to omens and prescient voices, and I had found their counsel to be meaningless. I therefore paid no attention to this nervous flutter,

125

and, as the shoe was passed to the Cuban exile, I bet a
second thousand against the bank and then stared pointedly across the table until the sum was matched by my
green enemy. My cards were snapped out of the shoe and
flipped toward me. I turned them over to reveal a count of
seven, a hand that requires no third card. The shill from
Havana produced a pair of aces for a total of two, and then
could do no better than augment this by the draw of a third
ace. The ten one-hundred-dollar bills that had been swept
away from me a minute before were now returned, and the
shoe was handed to the man whom I had chosen for personal combat. He started to push forward a stack of bills,
but then hesitated, a brief apology emanating from his eyes.
It was I who had begun challenging him, and he had
enough sense of ritual to know that he should wait for my
decision on the sum to be bet. My response to this unexpected courtesy was to let the thousand I had just won
remain with my original wager. The croupier acknowledged
the two-thousand-dollar bet and waited until a like amount
was placed in action by my opponent.

During the seconds it took him to do this, I sat with my
hands folded in front of me, hearing but not listening to
the salesman as he muttered adjurations for our good fortune. My own mind contained nothing but the image of the
brown box from which the cards would be drawn, and my
body, inwardly buzzing, appeared calm.

The cards arrived, sliding neatly in front of me from the
croupier's spatula. I unlocked my hands and turned them
over. A four and a three—a hand that signaled that I was
more than two-thirds on my way to triumph. And then my
opponent turned up two queens—a count of zero. He had to
draw, and the only cards that would save him were a seven
for a tie, and an eight or nine for a win. My victory was now
even closer. One card more and I would close a moment in

my life that had passed without a flaw and on which I could build further assaults upon Providence. Now my senses were opened: I could hear every sound in the casino, discern every face that was watching the play at the table. Especially, I saw the smiling lady. She had sensed the importance of the moment and had not bet, thus bestowing no favor on the combatants except that of her presence. As the card was drawn, I stared at her in a way that would forever join her to the moment. Then I glanced down at the card that would decide the hand just as the chief croupier called out its value.

It was an eight, and, in front of the spectators, in front of the salesman who had seconded me, in full view of the sulking Cuban and my punctilious opponent, in sight of the attentive serving-girl and the indifferent dealers, and in the presence of the lady whose smile might have been forever happily perpetuated in my memory—with all these as witnesses, I, only once, but with obvious petulance, struck the table with my hand. It was enough to see the lady's smile instantly fade to realize how this gesture had been generally received. And as I slid the offending hand from view, I knew also that whatever thread of good fortune I'd spun about me since arriving here had been snapped. This was as certain to me as the pain in my bowels, which now became torminous; and although a rational mind must insist that the grimace of a stranger or a moment of intestinal agony has no causal link to the way cards will fall, it is nevertheless true that a gambler's instinct comprehends relations between events that are perhaps too subtle for ordinary modes of observation. It is this instinct on which his survival is based, for if he ignores it and, while feeling disconnected from propitious flows and patterns, continues stubbornly to force a return of the good feeling he had about himself, he becomes nothing but an item of desperation, someone doomed to be unloved by fortune and destroyed by mathematics.

However, I did not appreciate this then. I was overwhelmed with shame at the manner in which I'd lost, but I hoped that one or two winning wagers would heal the wound I had inflicted on myself with that absurd thump on the table at the wrong turn of a card.

Of course, I continued to lose. The remaining cash in front of me went, as did, in clumps of three and four, the traveler's checks I'd purchased that morning. They also fled from me whom my time of good luck had attracted: first, the lady whose smile I had erased; then, while I was putting my signature on a fresh quartet of checks, without even a muttered farewell, my faithful peddler quit the field; and finally, the girl with ragged stockings, sensing rightly that my inclination toward grand gestures had passed, withdrew personal attendance. Only the Cuban shill remained constant, offering hollow encouragements as she watched me spiral downward toward the defeat that meant she'd done her job successfully.

This abandonment neither saddened nor angered me. All my energy was absorbed by the cards, which were remorselessly taking back everything I'd won since arriving in Las Vegas. Finally, there was nothing on the table or in my pockets left to lose, and I could only feebly signal an abstention when the cards were passed to me. I knew I had to withdraw, but I had been far too brutalized by bad fortune to consider returning to my room and disciplining myself with an accurate bookkeeping.

I rose, turned from the table, and, trying to posture dignity, made my way past the crowd surrounding me. Looking straight ahead, I continued on through the casino, knowing, but not admitting, what my destination was until I was there, in front of the cashier's window, waiting for my signature to be checked and my safety-deposit box brought to me. From behind his cage, the clerk I'd pitied the night before looked at me in a way that suggested he knew precisely what my condition was. He smiled, I thought, too courteously, and quickly disappeared into a small room where he would find the treasure I had only the night before stored away. While I stood there, I waited for something to restrain me, for a phrase or image that would come to mind and make me seem ridiculous to myself and let me end the evening safely wrapped in a sense of humor. But I was incapable of articulate thought, and my brain fashioned nothing for my salvation except bursts of gibberish that held reality at a distance while I waited for the clerk's return.

When he did, I signed two one-thousand-dollar traveler's checks, received their equivalent in cash, and returned to the casino. All of the sounds and images of chance were manifest: the hawking, the squeaks of pleasure, the trite craps-table imprecations, the blank stares of the enthralled, the whirrs and rattles of all the gaudy machines that measure luck. For a moment I thought of retreating, for as compelled as I was, I sensed that no one with a befuddled mind or wounded confidence should step into such a compassionless arena. However, in spite of this flash of misgiving, I allowed myself to be drawn into this early-morning rush toward success or exhaustion.

The session was not mercifully swift. Sitting at a blackjack table in one of the remote corners of the room, locked in place as transient players freely came and went, I was reduced by bits and pieces to a desperate seeker of good omens. Would, for instance, a lady, who hummed to herself while she played, bring me luck or anguish? Would the Indian in a beaded vest and smudged undershirt use his dark, speckled eyes to the table's advantage by casting spells

129

upon the dealer? Should I slip deeper into drunkenness so that, like the Persians described by Herodotus, I could dare to make more ambitious gambles?

When nothing external made the cards more favorable, I created incantations in my mind, semi-audible dronings that I hoped would protect me from further misfortune. Snatches of poetry, declensions of Latin nouns, the names of statesmen and movie stars—all were tested for magic, and all, after some success, proved to be false formulas. And so, as the room emptied in the early morning hours, I sat, disheveled and driven, mumbling imbecile phrases over the cards as they fell in front of me.

The casual player had long since left the room, and only those who were determinedly trying to increase or redeem their night's fortune hovered around the tables. None of these should have chosen mine for luck or respite. The overflowing ashtrays, my impatience with the dealers, the way, whether I'd won or lost the hand, I would smash a stack of chips in front of me—all this should have warned another gambler that mine was a table in distress. I was therefore surprised when, in the middle of a hand, I sensed someone slipping into the chair next to me and asking for a thousand-dollar credit slip. I waited until the hand was over and I had lost, then I looked darkly at the interloper who was now amiably chatting with the dealer.

I recognized the sagging juvenile features, especially the tiny pouting mouth that could twist itself into hundreds of shapes in order to add emphasis to the punchline of a joke and had always been used, therefore, as a peremptory signal for laughter. He had been a crude but forceful comedian who, before I embraced adult humor, had years ago made me laugh. But now he had fallen from the status of headliner to that of a subordinate lounge performer, a descent that indicated most of his audience had also outgrown him.

Nevertheless, though forced to share a stage with a Korean magician and to pander to an audience that, on its way back and forth from the gambling tables, dissolved and re-formed in the middle of his act, he was signing thousand-dollar markers as though they were no more than souvenir photographs for his admirers. Apparently, even though he had tumbled to a low show-business stratum, he was being paid well by the hotel's owners—a high-priced decoration that might make customers believe the casino was not devoted to one grim purpose. The night before I had watched him for a few moments as he finished his act, manfully telling jokes about morons, wives, the problems of middle-aged potency, and the antic details of his prostate condition. Hardly anyone had listened, and when he finished his act, the applause came mostly from waitresses and bartenders.

"Ted, you stone-faced bandit," he was talking to the dealer, who wore a nameplate over his heart, "give me another thousand. If I lose, I can use you as a tax deduction."

I looked at the comedian's face, mottled with moles and freckles, resting, as if neckless, atop a frilled dinner jacket of black and red velvet, and wished its owner dead. I was only a few hundred dollars away from losing all the cash the two checks had given me, and I was naturally reluctant to have this gaudy caricature of failure next to me, a fool who could do nothing to brighten the moment except drag out the exhausted one-liners that formed the standard banter of hopeless situations. An hour before, full of pride and self-esteem, I might have welcomed his ornate person in my entourage. But now there was too much that was fateful about him, too much of the crude, comic subplot that, as it mimics and mocks the embroilments and imperatives of tragedy, gives to all human existence a debasing unity that allows the groundling to affect a destiny in common with kings.

131

And so I waited, making minimum bets, hoping that the comedian's bad luck would drive him away to his demi-star's suite and leave me to struggle on without his professional merriment. However, no matter how much he lost, he seemed to have an infinite source of credit. More markers were signed, larger and larger bets were made, and, through it all, he kept up a banal monologue of quips and gaming-room homilies.

"If you play fast you can't last. If you play slow, you gotta go." This said in a W. C. Fields voice.

"If you smile when you lose, you have had too much booze." This sung to the opening strains of "The Star-Spangled Banner."

"If the dice ain't nice, you pay a price; if the cards run bad, we are gonna be sad." He directed this at me with an accompanying wink.

I looked stern and unamused, but since he'd grown used to cold receptions, he shrugged and, defiantly keeping his eyes on me, bubbled on.

"Don't worry, we can always come back next year and visit our money, for hard luck's better than no luck at all, which means you're dead or married to my wife's mother who can beat me at any game you can name for any amount that you can count, and after all it's not so bad to lose if you can get a deeper sense of poverty while doing so, which is what my grandmother meant when she said to me, 'Gladys,' she always thought I was a girl because I never left the toilet seat standing, 'when you bet on a sure thing always keep enough money to get home on,' a bit of advice that's wasted on gambling degenerates like us because we *are* home and would rather make a hard eight than fornicate, which is what the voice had in mind that kept whispering in the gambler's ear, 'eight on the big wheel, eight on the big wheel,' for two days, until the gambler comes back to

Vegas, puts all he has on eight, sees a sixteen come up and hears a voice say 'oh shit,' and so you learn that even God don't win at Las Vegas."

This was enough. I could no longer drag out the night's endgame after such a commentary. I bet the remainder of what I had taken from my deposit box and lost. The comedian clucked as the money was taken from me.

"Now thou art an o without a figure," I heard him say. "I am better than thou art now. I am a fool, thou art nothing."

Of course, he did not speak these words. I was merely shielding myself with a final bit of grandiloquent drama. All the notions and images that had that night cluttered my head—the Sir Gawain-at-the-gaming-table tableau, featuring the Fair Lady, a *belle dame sans merci,* one Green Knight, comic Squire, and the fateful mortal flaw (my petulant thump on the table)—and that I have recorded because I was, in fact, fanciful enough to dally with them in a dangerous situation, were giving way to an unadorned view of myself as someone whose journey of great expectation was close to being over. And so I tried another pretense, and was Lear with only the punishing words of my fool for comfort as I fled from the blackjack table.

However, by the time I had walked the gauntlet of slot machines that led to the casino's elevator, the ability to costume honest fact and feeling left me. Now it seemed that my pain had no antecedents, no history in common with anything produced by past imagination. For the thousandth time in my life I learned that there were no fixed categories of distress for a healthy ego, no matter how fine its cultivation.

It was again dawn when I entered my room, but I found nothing this time exhilarating about the early desert light. Rather, it increased the fear I was struggling to control, making me feel out of joint with the natural cycle of things. The data of the past night danced upon my nerves, and, attending to the details of undressing, I used all the wiles left me—incoherent chatter and manic laughter—to make sport of my predicament.

But I could not for long occlude my true feelings. Perched naked on the edge of the bed in which I had romped just twenty-four hours ago with a pert, maidenly whore, my arms wrapped around my damp torso, I heard myself moan, the sound rumbling through my chest and rising slowly into a rough, glottal cry. It was a vile, depressing noise, which could not be stifled and which sent painful vibrations through the length of my body. Bit by bit, as I sat keening on the hotel bed, the night re-formed in my mind. I flinched at each image, whined aloud for a chance to relive with more prudence the moments that had cost me my self-assurance, and twisted finally into a fetal coil when I imagined my present condition viewed by all those who would relish its agonies.

For they were on hand, the faces of those injured by my life, floating in the room, beaming over my naked writhings on a hotel bed. Spirits that were not to be propitiated with petty degradations, they fed on my pride until they were swollen with triumph; and I could do nothing but meekly endure their joys and smug vengeance.

Youthful faces that I had not seen for twenty years looked down on me like malevolent cherubs and teasingly recalled how I had always made them aware that I felt my life was going to be of greater consequence than theirs; a trio of women, who had been the victims of my youthful suspicion of human feeling, became cackling Graeae in the corner of my room, their single eye merrily focused on my limpness; a novelist whom I had, in print, accused of being a flaccid moralist, drifted by me smirking satisfaction; friends whom I had worn out and discarded sternly approved the price I was now paying for self-sufficiency; and dozens of others, less distinct but not less painful, on whom my life had thrown a shadow, whom I had patronized, swindled, made sport of or insulted, had their moment of retribution.

I rose from the bed and began pacing furiously. I still embraced myself, trying to hold my body together while spasms and palpitations concussed it. Gradually, after a dozen turns around my suite, the phantoms began to recede, but they left behind them an aching fear that, like so many voyages in my past, this one would wear itself out, without providing any vital discoveries about the world, or my place in it.

It is an earlier and brighter morning in my life. I am in the back seat of a taxi that is moving down the east side of Manhattan. From my window, I can look across the river and see the borough I grew up in, and, like the early summer haze, my youth hangs over the billboards and factories that line the Queens-side shore of the river. I feel no sorrow at leaving my past suspended there, for my memories have not yet ripened into poignancy. Moreover, I feel the world is all before me, that I have finally escaped from the duties and constricting affections of youth. Although still no patriot, I am off to join my country's army and perhaps take part in its war against the Republic of North Korea. This seems the simplest way to discover my capacity to meet life on adult terms, and I am ready to risk even death on an Oriental peninsula if it means that I need no longer wait to take up the world's serious and passionate business.

Six months later and a darker morning. I am standing in a cold rain in front of the Personnel Office at Camp Chaffee, Arkansas. I am disgusted and wear a devious expression.

Military life has so far created in me only a shallow desire for minimal comforts and a brutish sense of survival. The examples of war that I have been trained in are dull and fatiguing, and I have long since given up the notion, which I never held very strongly, that death's proximity will produce anything of great value to me. I do not wish to risk stumbling half-consciously into oblivion or even successfully to endure the inevitable bad weather of combat. And so I stand, with a chastened imagination, in the Arkansas rain, waiting for a fellow New Yorker to adjust my records so that I will be able to transfer to a more accommodating branch of service. As I shall so often in the future, I am using the problems of language to my advantage. I am off to become a polyglottal member of military intelligence.

Now, a third-rate spy, I am in front of a bombed-out Frauenkirche in Frankfurt. My stay in Germany, besides bringing me into contact, in my position as Civilian Personnel Investigator, with a few ex-Nazis and a great many woebegone but decent leftovers from Hitler's Reich, has provided me with an untutored passion for church architecture and a clinical sophistication in the ways of gonorrheal infection. I am in such a dual condition now, the leakage from infected genitals dampening my crotch as I stare enraptured at the church's broken façade. I have been to Cologne, Nuremberg, Lübeck, Ulm and a dozen other cities to stare at spires, buttresses, socles and vaults, about which I know nothing except that they stir up in me imprecise desires for a rich and complex faith. I have had, since my alliance with Gino, no such belief and am still ignorant in the fundamentals necessary to create one. I am forced therefore to put my troubled soul again and again in the hands of infected Rhinemaidens.

And so I return to New York, my system purified by modern drugs, my mind clotted with undigested thoughts and images. The journey has been premature, and I now understand that one must have more knowledge than I do at present in order to master the complex details of the world. Also, I have come to know, through my dealings with the defeated, the danger of ignorance, of being overwhelmed by untutored aspiration. I must learn, therefore, to be articulate about my desires. Vague throbbings in front of a lunette or next to the daughter of a defunct Nazi official will no longer suffice. The Army has taught me a few elementary tricks of survival. However, in order to understand what I am surviving for, I dutifully begin to study.

It is the second voyage remembered in the Las Vegas morning. I am now an accredited scholar bound for further studies in Europe. It is a hot August afternoon and I am sitting with Edward, my traveling companion, on the Spanish Steps in Rome. Around us are chattering students, tourists and complacent Italians. Edward and I both lounge with youthful insolence atop Bernini's creation and are appropriately caustic about the goings-on around us. At apposite moments we quote Catullus, Michelangelo, Petrarch and Martial, happy to be at the very center of our history.

Suddenly Edward, the young man from Newark, stands and shouts the refrain from the *"Pervigilium Veneris."*

Cras amet qui nunquam amavit quique amavit cras amet rings out through the Piazza di Spagna. Everyone looks blankly at Edward except one young man with matted hair, sallow skin, and several missing teeth. He undulates up the stairs toward us and smiles at Edward.

"Perchè domani?" he asks, his tongue slipping in and out through the gaps in his teeth. I am taken aback, but Edward laughs. He finds out the young man's name is Mario, and he invites him to accompany us on a visit to the house in which Keats died.

When I first met Edward, he was often hysterical and

subject to fits of depression over his growing awareness that he was a homosexual. But he was also brilliant and rich with feelings that seemed identical to my own. At first, I was merely curious about his sexual anguish and his precise, self-mocking manner, but gradually, as our friendship deepened, I began wishing that I, too, could affect such a cultivated agony. Next to Edward, I seemed a crude voluptuary, and, inspired by our many frank conversations, in which he drew strength from the Socratic vision and I displayed my ability to refute the hypostatic moralists, I began to be curious about what would happen if I simply let our friendship evolve into love. When Edward sensed one day that I was thinking of such a pact between us, he startled me by crying, and promising that he would bow to my moods in the delicate matter of consummation.

And so he did, until we arrived in Europe, he bound for Oxford, I off to the University of Munich. We had three summer months before taking up our studies, and, beginning in Spain, we worked our way slowly along the Mediterranean coast, lying in the sun, talking about our futures, and feeling as limitless as the blue southern sky we traveled under. However, by the time we reached Rapallo, some of the holiday exultation had left Edward, and was replaced by a waspish tone of innuendo that seemed strongest following the very moments when we were both moved, by a particular view or edifice, to exclamations of gratitude that we were sharing such things together.

Sensitive to this shift in mood, I allowed Edward to lie with me, but I found that the flesh cannot be bullied by philosophy or desire created through cold experiments.

After a few minutes of tepid fondling, Edward desisted and looked darkly amused.

"I won't rudely force you," he said.

We were, I knew, going to banter half-truths for a while. I hoped for nothing deeper.

"After all, we know and love each other. We aren't engaged in a sordid little *pissoir* intrigue, I can go on being patient, but only if . . ."

He stopped and looked at the floor, still smiling.

"Only if?"

"If I'm not something you're using to dabble in evil with. Don't look shocked. As an apostate of the Holy Church, I know when a sense of sin is making itself felt. A sour presence. I can almost smell it. It rose out of you as soon as we touched. You who when drunk compare yourself to Genghis Khan, have something like the odor of old moralities about you. What was it Pope called one of his contemporaries? 'A vile antithesis?' Well, Jack, I don't think you're vile, but you are antithetical."

Despite the pain of Edward's insight, I tried to keep the moment fixed in a tone of light academic debate.

"Only the gods accept everything," I said. " '*Nec pro bene capitur . . .*' "

Edward flinched.

"First get the quotation straight. '*Nec bene pro meritus capitur, nec tangitur Ira!*' I give you John Wilmot's translation: 'Not pleased by Good Deeds; nor provoked by Bad.' By which Lucretius meant that the gods were indifferent to human actions, not that they accepted them. Now since I love you I certainly don't want your indifference; I assume your acceptance. What would be intolerable is your forgiveness."

Edward had spoken sincerely and passionately. I could not accept that there was fraudulence in my feelings for him. Instead, I laughed and feigned contrition. I protested that, if I did harbor notions of sin, it was because, in a benighted state, I had spent too much time lost among the gloom of Gothic architecture.

But I was wrong to blame the Gothic style. Now, on my knees, I am moving up the baroque Scala Santa in the church of San Salvatore. Next to me, halfway through her climb, an old woman is wheezing invocations and manipulating her beads. Each step demands for her a full rosary, and, since the marble has already caused my knees to ache, I wonder about hers, and whether she will successfully reach the end of her penitential crawl.

Two steps above me, side by side, Edward and Mario are whispering together and smothering thin bursts of laughter. All afternoon, even as we stood next to the bed in which Keats died, they have been engaged in cultural coquetry, using everything from bits of fascist rhetoric to statuary penes as fuel for their flirtation. And now these holy stairs, each step of which promises indulgence, have become part of their ritual, and their witty, improvised prayers challenge me as definitely as do the by-rote dronings of the woman who shares my step.

Finally, they reach the end of their mocking ascent. Edward turns and looks down from the top of the staircase. He smiles and beckons me to hurry, but then catches something in my expression that causes the smile to fade. As he watches, I move one step higher and stop, as if I were keeping to the crippling pace of the old woman who, though again next to me, is oblivious of my presence. Edward's eyes flash with anger, and he turns and descends an unsanctified staircase with his Roman *tapette*. I watch them step through the portal past a dozing priest into the late-afternoon sunlight.

That night, supposing that Mario has kept his promise to take my friend on a nighttime cruise of the Forum, I go off alone to frolic with the ladies of the Baths of Caracalla. When we meet later in our room, Edward and I are cordial, but we decide dryly that our trip is over and that we should head for our different universities.

"By the way," Edward asks after some silence, "who won the race to the top of the stairs, you or the *signora?*"

"We arrived together, a dead heat."

Edward smiles and then goes to stare out of the window. Except for the steady splash of fountain water, the square beneath our room is still. Edward yawns and then sadly shakes his head.

"You know," he says softly, "you looked idiotic on those stairs, enjoying the vicarious thrill of humility."

Edward shudders and rubs his arms as if cold. He closes the shutters and comes to sit next to me on the small pension bed.

"You don't know what that toothless minion took me to. What smells and ugliness. To be sodomized upon an antique plinth while the lover next in line empties his bladder in front of you, does not produce a feeling of heroic defiance."

"What happened? I thought . . ."

"You thought?" Edward snaps. "You thought I was off with some pathetic street urchin? A harmless example of Italian poverty that happened to know Latin? That's all you saw? I was his rich American fairy for the day. He and the rest of his band meet each night and, after a bit of preliminary robbery, keep the most fetching among their catches on for a little sport."

Edward stops, and for a moment the only sound is the rush of his breathing.

"I didn't know. I'm sorry." As I say this, I am trying not to see too vividly what he has described.

"You're sorry?" Edward says. "Didn't you know what I was doing? Couldn't you tell all I wanted was a sign that I mattered to you? I wanted you to be outraged over the caricature I was making of myself."

"You mean," I say calmly, as though helping him with a problem in semantics, "you wanted me to be jealous."

"All right then, jealous. Yes, you could have been that. What after all do you think love is? Of course I wanted to provoke you. Not in order to crawl into your bed, but just to feel that I could expect more from you than a desire to caress my soul from time to time. What were you using me for, Jack? All this time, what in God's name did you mean by love? A college prank? A literary experience? Or was it really just a chance for you to feel sinful, to be a moral thrill seeker?"

I answer nothing. I understand his charges in the same way I have understood the consequences of our friendship. With exquisite miscomprehension, I am more pained on his behalf than on my own. I reach out to take his hand, but Edward jumps up from the bed and switches on the light.

"My dear Jack," he says, in a vicious imitation of coquetry, "what kind of overture *are* you making? After all, I've just enjoyed a whole Forumful of boys. I'm simply *épuisé*, darling."

I start to protest, but Edward responds with a look that precludes any further exchange between us. Then, in his own voice, he asks me to leave the room. When I look puzzled, he explains.

"I have some administering to do to myself. I wasn't treated gently by Mario and his friends. I don't want to soil your memory of Rome any more than I already have."

I am not insensitive enough to offer assistance. I leave and, for several hours, walk through the streets of Rome. I look at nothing, afraid that everything Edward has said about me would be confirmed should I become interested in the carvings on a palace façade or the design of a neoclassical fountain. When I return to our room, I find Edward has packed and gone, leaving nothing behind except a picture of us that had been taken a week before by a street photographer in Florence. I spend the rest of the night thinking about his agony, relieved somewhat that he is no longer there to personify it.

In the morning I set off for my studies in Munich. As I stated in my fellowship application, I intend to reconcile aspects of logical empiricism with the principles of modern phenomenology. I effect no such reconciliation, and in less than a year return to New York to take up marriage and begin a career.

There had been many other trips that came to hollow ends, but my mind was no longer capable of reliving them in a Las Vegas hotel room. To preserve itself from further pain, it grew blank—except for one thought that has always courted my favor by offering me a certain amount of tawdry comfort. It was the concept of my own insignificance that whorishly consoled me, the principle that what I did or suffered was really of small consequence when matched against the failure of life itself to be coherent. A corollary of that forgiveness which Edward spoke of, this idea rises when one, facing defeat, takes the larger view of things, fixes the mind on final causes, and makes of the details of life trifles that can only interest the ignorant and the shortsighted.

This moment of reflection, which stopped my trembling, was the final degradation of the night, and with it, my descent ended. For several minutes I lay in resignation, but then, slowly, prompted by disgust at the level of consolation to which I'd sunk, I began to revive. It was now well into morning, and with the brightening sunlight came small bursts of anger over the amount of chastisement I had brought into my room with me. It was definitely a time for careful restoration. First, I phoned for breakfast to be sent me, and, while waiting its arrival, stood under a shower, alternating hot and cold streams of water, until I felt the stirrings of some carnal exhilaration and a passable appetite. When the food came, I ate with deliberation, making sure I recognized the enjoyment that could be had from eggs flecked with pepper, evenly buttered, jam-covered toast, and hot black coffee.

Having attended to the flesh, I turned to the more difficult task of reviving the spirit. Contempt, disappointment, memories of failure and self-indulgence—all these had to be dealt with. Of course, I had suffered their effects before, but never, it seemed, with such clarity, or with such fear that they were more than temporary discomforts. I had always believed that whatever I did was capable, some day, somehow, of redemption. Now, however, it was time to admit that, regardless of my end, I would live not as an unmarked child of fortune, but as someone who, in spite of weakness and errors, wins a happy fate for himself. No matter if I force a moment of vileness upon a lady and cause her smile to fade; or become, for a time in my mind, the butt of a comedian's ridicule; or cringe in front of ghosts who remind me that I have loved badly. No matter if I pose, inveigle, prey, blaspheme, read private runes or think that civilization itself hangs in the balance when I await the result of a hand at blackjack. No matter all this, for I am neither a cipher without a figure nor any longer a delicate voyeur. I am, I believe, at the heart of things that matter, and whatever I risk, whatever I am forced to reveal about myself, will be easy payment should I obtain the guerdon I desire.

Having thus roused myself to meet the day, I slipped into a bathing suit and went down to the hotel's pool. The sun was already fierce, and tanning bodies were scattered about the poolside lawn. I lay down among them, and although this was my first real exposure to the desert sun, disdained oils or ointments. Supine, my arms and legs spread apart, I welcomed the rays and willed that they not harm me.

I knew that later I would have to return to my room, take up my bookkeeping, and decide on future strategies commensurate with my reduced finances. But for now, I wanted to experience nothing except simple solar warmth and energy.

Chapter VII

$$\sim (\exists x) \ x = x$$

I wrote the above formula while I was a student of philosophy in Munich. My enthusiasm for my subject, which had at one time stirred in me a wish to distill and define the universe, was almost exhausted, and I was becoming, due to a spreading positivistic infection, a morbid enemy of speculative thought, determined that if I could not slip past my own refutations into glory, no one else would.

$\sim (\exists x) \ x = x$, however, filled me with a demented sense of possibility. The formula seemed at the moment of its conception to be a legitimate way of describing Nothing, Nullity, Nothingness or any of the other theatrical concepts of total absence of matter and spirit, human or divine. For translated into English, the symbols mean that there is no thing identical with itself, or, more bluntly, there are no things. I had therefore found a way to state, in the wry form of a logical proposition, an alternative to the clutter of entities on which philosophy had wasted so much time.

This achievement was of consequence to me because, as betrayed as I felt I'd been by every philosopher who'd promised me proof that I and the world were more than dreams or accidents, I did not want to see philosophy, like astrology and alchemy, demoted to the status of an historical curio. Indeed, I'd come to Germany in the hope that I might salvage something usable from the old traditions of thought, that I might learn to trust again in sentences that offered more to the spirit than tidy syntax and simple verification. Day after day, in seminars on esthetics, phenomenology, epistemology, ethics and metaphysics, I'd force myself to listen sympathetically to philosophy performed in high, idealistic German style, to nouns and verbs desperately compounding themselves as they strained to become definitions that would unify thought and matter, time and space, beauty and truth, and the rest of the old dualities that once gave philosophy its high moments of intellectual tension. As generous as I tried to be toward these attempts to speak majestically about the world, I heard nothing that made me believe that there were truths larger than those expressed in sentences like "At a certain time and place it is probable that I perceived green." After a while I stopped attending classes and began a private purge of those philosophers whose errors I considered the most dangerous to an honest state of mind.

I did not begin cautiously. The first to be banished was the aristocrat Plato, the philosopher who'd created the noblest vision of mind, matter and soul of any thinker with a private income and a taste for worldly pleasure. However, he had founded this sublime view of things on a terrible error; namely, the belief that tautologies are evidence of the mind's possession of necessary truths. For anyone who's been

147

fascinated by his own thoughts, this is indeed a seductive notion, for it offers leisurely enjoyment of one's own logic, a peaceful apprehension of truths that have no need of commerce with the low-bred disorders of the external world. However, in its isolation from the rough ambiguities of life's surfaces, all the Platonic mind can do is make up new geometries and games for itself, and all it can commune with are the minds born to share its premises. Faced with the question whether a man ought to be crucified for disturbing the peace or whether sex three times a day is morally good or bad, such minds are helpless, for they must find answers consistent with the axioms they have made up for the sake of a coherent world, but in those very axioms are the questions they wish to answer. Thus Plato's dialectic, so exalted in its Socratic personification, was nothing more than intelligence discovering over and over again its own hypothesis and then exulting in the impossible task of turning the hypothetical into reality. It had all made for marvelous talk, for exquisite demonstrations that a heaven of pure passion and ideal proportions is self-evident to those with a knack for philosophy. But it had all been done with tricks, with arithmetic illusions and logical mirrors that had dazzled me for a time, but now seemed shoddy devices to make the world thinkable.

But it was not easy to exile Plato, especially in Munich during the last days of October, since this is the time that the city celebrates, with unabashed grossness, the existence of beer. My window looked out on the meadow where each of the local breweries had erected a mammoth tent in which, accompanied by brass bands, the *Müncheners* could drink the local product from foot-high steins decorated with slightly obscene *Sprichwörter* on the pleasures and problems of drink. The celebrants, weaving and groaning, often converted the rich Bavarian brews into urine or vomit beneath my window, and I would watch them sadly, my gaze gradually rising to the dark October sky from which I had chased all exquisite forms and absolutes. I longed to glimpse there, through sense or intuition, something finer than a Bavarian beer festival, something beyond a life of *Oktoberfests*. But I apprehended nothing, and Plato gave way finally before a lederhosened Hans Wurst who, in his human excesses, required no subtle proof of his existence.

Aristotle, with his categories, followed his mentor into exile, for he had been no less guilty of trimming the world to suit his philosophy. Some Cynics, Stoics and Epicureans I allowed to linger, since they had generally not presumed to tell the truth about life, merely to state a few useful hints for getting through it. Church Fathers and theologians who had played with ontological, causal or teleological proofs received notices of eviction; those who had urged humility and faith, I kept in reserve in case it ever came to pass that the only course left open to me was that of an exhausted conversion.

A few days before Christmas came the hardest parting of all. I had truly admired Descartes; the range of his thought was impressively contained, the method of his inquiry an expanding spiral of taut induction. Even if he had fallen back on the idea of an undeceitful god in order to verify the world's reality, it was a small indulgence that one allowed him in gratitude for his establishing the indubitableness of the ego, of the thinking subject that may doubt everything except the fact that it is indeed doubting. His *Cogito, ergo sum* had been much more to me than a philosophical catchword; it was, if one examined it with care and understanding, an exquisite monstrance in which a radiant human Self was revealed. However, I had learned from the history of logic that what is not needed need not be. From Occam's Razor to Sheffer's Stroke, the principle of refinement and reduction had been the duty of thought, and with sadness I admitted that "I think, therefore I am" was just a dramatic way of saying that "There are thoughts." Ergo, there is no logical reason to believe that one's thoughts are one's own, any more than there is reason to believe that one's perceptions are containers of reality. Descartes' attempt to prove his existence had been gallant, but even in a world of clear and distinct ideas, he was, by his own logic, a superfluity.

Kant, the champion of synthetic *a priori* space and time, had given me moments of hope that there might be a bit of noble immanence in the human mind. But I should have guessed from the beginning that anyone who resurrects the bureaucratic notion of categories, or who posits a *Ding-an-sich* whenever the phenomenal world gets out of hand, was not to be trusted. I realized that unlearned awareness of space and time was not a proof of intuitive knowledge but simply a primitive criterion for being alive. To say that one must be breathing in order to learn mathematics is to say enough to be condemned.

Just before Lent, after a mass trial of British Empiricists, I renounced my last connection with formal philosophy. Mathematics, not as a science of information but as an exquisite form of intellectual play, had become my refuge from the traducements of the senses. From the work of Cantor, Boole, Piano, Frege and Russell, I had drawn the conclusion that there could at least be imagined constructions of thought that pretended to nothing except their own consistency and completeness. Worn-out with looking for a workable nexus between mind and matter, I'd thought of counting myself among those about whom Poincaré said, "*La matière ne leur importe pas, la forme seule les intéresse.*" The forms in question were not those of Plato, a *ne plus ultra* chair or trapezoid floating in celestial ether and waiting patiently to be contemplated by the right philosopher.

Rather, they were strategies of mind, elaborate postulated edifices that needed no earthbound models or appeals to intuition for their proofs. They were complete, finished mosaics of intelligence that could not even be described by ordinary language, so magnificently useless was their esthetic appeal. I became, therefore, metalingual, thinking and speaking inside inverted commas, and for a time, confident that this new source of delight was infinite in its resources, I had been an addicted abstract thinker.

Then came Gödel's Proof, an infamous and arcane piece of brilliance that demonstrated that all axiomatic systems are incomplete, that they are condemned to be submitted to rules of inference whose consistency must always be in doubt. For a long time I resisted the grim argument that ran through Gödel's definitions and lemmata, willfully refusing to understand the conclusions I sensed they led to. All I now had left were a few algebraic standards and I had no intentions of parting with them easily, of admitting that there was no worthwhile mental enterprise that was above suspicion.

However, determined to end the purge without sentiment, I reluctantly sentenced the mathematicians to return, as they seemed ready to do, to Platonic Realism and there to waste precious time in the search for ideal numbers. This last judgment came as the pre-Lenten holiday in Munich was ending, when the streets were filled with costumed revelers swaying and singing through the night. Secure in the anonymity of carnival motley, they kissed and fondled each other roughly, laughed, belched and copulated in celebration of their mortality and the belief that, no matter what their excesses, they would be pardoned and redeemed. Dressed as a French matelot, I goosed and howled with the others through the last days of *Fasching*, and on the morning before Ash Wednesday, I awoke in Munich's English

Gardens, with dozens of others who had passed out the night before, and accepted, with help from a hangover, my unverifiable self as the fragile arbiter of all inconstant things in a slightly probable world.

I should say almost accepted. Old habits were hard to put away, and flashes of thought kept returning to entice me back into quests for a systematic life. $\sim(3x) \; x = x$ was one of these last throbs of speculation, and for several weeks, I actually thought that by starting with a logic whose model would be nothing, a logic whose first theorem implied its uniqueness, I might come to the truth about the world through its negation. I nurtured my formula through the spring, taking it with me on trips to the mountains, weighing its logical force against the Bavarian scenery, its decree of emptiness against the Alps' inconclusive beauty.

With summer, however, sanity returned, and I saw that what I'd considered unique about my proposition rendered it a useless contradiction. For if $\sim(3x) \; x = x$ itself were a singular instance, then of course it must be considered to exist, whether as a logical concept or as a sensible phenomenon. This time, as I stared into paradox, I vowed never again to think formally about anything that mattered, or worry that I hadn't earned the right to express anger at, and snatch relative pleasure from, a universe that tolerates no sincere predicates.

I have recounted this erosion of belief because what follows is a moral narrative, and I want it understood that I was supported by no body of principles that I felt transcended my own patched-together character.

For days after I had lost more than a third of all the money I possessed, I courageously fought back all doubts about my being unfit for a gambler's life and continued to return to the tables. I wandered from casino to casino, betting small amounts now and then at craps or blackjack, waiting for a sign of encouragement, a brief run of luck that would justify doubling or tripling my betting units until I was in a position to recover in an instant everything I'd lost. And, indeed, there were flurries here and there of good fortune, but they never lasted long enough for me to feel the confidence needed for increased commitment, and I would wait until the dice or cards turned against me and then wander off feeling that my reluctance had been justified. I thought I was displaying admirable self-control, but I was really afraid to face the risk of a large gamble, to submit again to the full force of chance and to feel my entire being at stake in the encounter. Sleeping in snatches, always restless, unable to sit still long enough to eat anything that took longer than a hamburger to prepare, I traversed miles of gambling space, stopping only now and then to make a furtive bet or to peer diffidently over the shoulders of other players.

I was, of course, paying a high price for vacillation. By betting amounts that could not quickly bring me even, I subjected myself to the steady attrition of the house percentage. In a few days of caution, I had frittered away nearly a thousand dollars, and the time came when I could no longer pretend that I was acting with professional restraint, that I was not stultified by panic.

I decided therefore to economize, to move downtown to a cheaper hotel, to play in less plush casinos. I did not think of this change of surroundings as a discipline or a penance. Indeed, I felt that I would be more at ease in surroundings that made no attempt to soften the facts of gambling, to pretend that waiting for a wheel to stop or a card to be drawn was a holiday diversion. On the Strip, an appearance of fun and triviality is kept up by player and management, but downtown, along Fremont Avenue, where the casinos spill out into the street, and where, waiting for a bus or while buying the week's groceries, one's luck can be tested on slot machines and chuck-a-luck wheels, there is no effort made to keep gambling from becoming the main pattern of life. Here a player need not be ashamed to reveal that he is serious and fearful, for it is as though everyone in downtown Las Vegas understood that their survival in a world of accidents was not assured, and the woman who works the handle of a slot machine in eight-hour shifts, the dollar dice-player who times his appearance at the tables so that it coincides with the bar's free-drink hour, the clerks and taxi drivers who reduce their life's adventure to a standing lunch spent at the roulette wheels—all accept that they are in a *sauve-qui-peut* situation and tolerate any behavior that does not directly threaten their hope for sudden rescue.

I chose a hotel whose lobby was filled with sleeping cowboys and a few dazed women who read comic books or fed babies while their men were off at the tables trying to win the fare back home, or at least enough to pay the rent for a few more days. I was shown to my room by a thin, pale, weary-looking young man, who was as uninterested in the process of my checking-in as I was. He delivered a quick speech on the virtues of the women he could procure, and then left, leaving the door open behind him, as if he knew I would be following in a few seconds. And in just that amount of time I was out in the streets, heading for casinos with sawdust floors, faro tables, and wheels of chance that had been spinning since this part of America had been settled. Indeed, as you walk off the street through swinging doors and enter these rough, informal rooms, you feel you've returned to a time when there was little else to do except gamble, when wages might as well be spent on cards and whiskey since there was nothing to buy, either for pleasure or out of need, that would make the coming year easier than the last.

If you do not actually find, clustered at the tables and bars, besotted miners, garrulous drummers, half-wild hunters, and cowboys cutting cards for an Indian whore, you do meet their descendants: wispy, less vivid specimens perhaps, but all wearing the blank, fugitive expression of the frontier.

"Can I buy you a drink, young fellow?"

It had been so long since anyone except a casino dealer had talked to me, that I didn't answer, certain that the man was addressing someone else. I kept staring at my reflection in the giant mirror behind the Lucky Horseshoe's bar, marveling how, in slightly over a week, I had become a study in genteel decline. Expensive suit, but unpressed and spotted; rumpled shirt with collar open and twisted over the jacket's lapels; face washed but unshaven; hair neat in appearance but really made rigid by sweat; expression, that of dignified hysteria, with eyes reflecting exhaustion.

"You don't look that good that you should pass up a drink."

This time I knew I was being spoken to. I looked at the man and said that I agreed with him.

"Blake's the name," he said. "Boris Blake, the last of a breed. Take a good look at me, young man, for I'm vanishing quickly."

I did and saw a comically malevolent face whose most impressive feature was a widow's peak that dropped across the width of his forehead almost to the bridge of the nose. The rest of his ink-black hair was slicked down on either side of a gleaming part that seemed made with a ruler. His eyes were slightly slanted, as were the brows above them. A thin mustache formed a neat triangle with his upper lip, and needed only a curl at each end to complete the standard portrait of a melodrama villain.

"So, are you taking out any money?" he asked when the drinks arrived. "You look like you've been working hard."

Even his voice had a twang of theatrical evil to it, a mixture of sinister cackles and greasy whines. His hands, however, were not those of a heartless landlord or riverboat sharper, not tapered and diabolically delicate. They were gruesomely large, with giant spatulate fingers into which the nails were crushed and embedded. They seemed deformed, yet they manipulated the drink and cigarette they held with unusual grace.

"This town is tough, I'm telling you. You don't get an inch from anyone here," Boris complained when I told him that things had not been going too well. "You look like a nice, gentlemanly person, if you know what I'm saying. And there's nothing around here but a bunch of thieves."

"All the thieves are on the house side of the table," I said, hoping that Boris was off on a loser's lament. To coax someone else who has lost into a display of chagrin is one of the lowest forms of comfort available to a losing gambler, but I was not above making use of it.

"You understand me," Boris said, a bit of amazement in his voice, as if he'd said something terribly complex. "You come here for a little honest gambling and you have to make yourself a sucker, turn yourself into a mark before they let you play. You gotta walk around carrying their vig on your back like some sort of coolie. Everyone's supposed to be equal in this country, so how come the house gets a five percent edge at blackjack and only pays thirty-to-one on double sixes?"

"That's the entertainment tax," I answered.

Boris reared back, his features arched in shock.

"And you're being entertained?" he asked.

At this point we suddenly were joined by the chief of the casino guards, a huge man who wore a gun and a serious expression.

"You're not thinking of doing any gambling here, are you, Boris?" he said softly. Boris put his glass down and asked why he was always being picked on every time he came into the Lucky Horseshoe, especially since he had lost thousands over the years at its tables.

When the guard answered with a blank expression, Boris demanded once and for all that it be explained to him why he should be hounded and harassed when he had the urge to make a five-dollar bet or just sniff around the games a little. Had he ever been offensive or slowed down the play at the tables? Was his money counterfeit, his breath bad, his racial origins not suited to the clientele's tastes? Was he, and he used this word with obvious pride in having learned it, a pariah? It seemed Boris could have continued his offended performance forever, but then he had to pause for breath and the hiatus in his complaint was filled by a drawled order to finish his drink and leave. Then the guardian of the casino patted him heavily on the back, stared at me for several seconds, and wandered off.

"I am *not* going to fool with crazy Texans," Boris said and drained his glass. "They're worse than the Wops up on the Strip. Up there they don't want to hurt anybody because of their image. Around here, they don't have any image that doesn't go with shooting people. It's their goddamn tradition, so I'm leaving."

During the next few days, as I waited for my luck to change, I kept glimpsing Boris prowling about the gambling rooms. Although he never bet or even mixed with the other players, he invariably was invited to leave by someone of menacing dimensions, and, after a brief argument, would quickly vanish.

I wondered vaguely why he was an outcast in a world open to anyone disposed to make a one-dollar bet, but I was too concerned with my own persecution to make any inquiries about his. The move to downtown Las Vegas was proving ineffective. In between bursts of luck, I still suffered long series of losses, and each morning I returned to my room three or four hundred dollars poorer than I'd been when the day began. With a brain filled with sour memories and sad financial calculations, it was impossible to sleep deeply, and I often simply forced myself to stay in bed until enough time had passed for me to believe that I must have rested. Then I'd jump up, splash water on my face, make a half-hearted effort to dry-shave—I was too impatient to be out of the room to bother with lathering—pick out my most presentable shirt, and head for the streets and another day at the tables.

I was eating lunch at a chili stand when I spoke to Boris the second time. For a day or so I had been unable to keep my hands from trembling whenever they closed in a gripping position, and I was having a difficult time trying to lead a huge, dripping taco into my mouth.

"Appearance is man's greatest asset, so said my uncle the tailor."

Boris was looking at a rivulet of rust-colored sauce oozing down my sleeve. I dabbed at it with a paper napkin and sent more of the taco splattering on the floor.

"They still grinding you out, young man?" he asked, taking a small but pointed step back from my droppings.

"Why do you keep calling me 'young fellow' and 'young man'?" I asked, trying to rise above my run-down condition.

"Just a manner of speaking," Boris protested. "Just a little friendly patter."

He paused and looked around him, his head throbbing forward and back like a lizard's.

"One of the few joints they don't throw me out of," he said approvingly. "Because it's one of the few joints that don't even have a slot machine on the premises."

I gave him a moment to savor his bitterness and then asked why he was so coolly received everywhere he went.

"Because I'm not a sucker," he answered proudly; then ruefully, "and because I've got too much heat. That's what I want to talk to you about, before they suck so much out of you that you start turning into a lush or shooting a little consolation up into your veins."

"I'm not so simple," I answered, and threw what remained of my Mexican lunch into a trashcan.

"I know you're not," Boris said, moving a little closer to me now that there was no danger of his being spattered. "I've got a good eye for class, and you look like you could move in any circles you wanted to. But let's face it, it don't look like you're doing too great at the moment."

"What if I'm not? Why should that interest you?"

"So you can tell I'm not an eccentric millionaire looking for people to help," Boris laughed. "The fact is, I've got a proposition for you if you can spare a little time. And in a way I am going to give you something for nothing. I am going to make you my heir."

We walked a block or so together and then got into a large station wagon. In a few minutes we were driving outside of Las Vegas, along a highway, through the desert.

"I mean this is bleak land, isn't it?" Boris sighed as we drove through a landscape of scrub cactus, dried clay, dust-covered rocks and tumbleweeds. "I was driving along a

159

highway through country like this in New Mexico once, and I kept seeing signs that read 'Beware of Gusts.' I've no idea what the hell a gust's supposed to be, so I figure you've got to be pretty hard luck to run into one. So don't you know one of those goddamn gusts comes up behind me when I'm doing seventy an hour, and flips my car right off the road. One lousy gust cost me three months in a hospital. I tell you, nature can be a mean son-of-a-bitch. Don't fool with it."

"Where are we going?" I asked, as Las Vegas began to recede behind us.

"Somewhere where I can make you my offer in private," Boris said, and after chuckling and muttering to himself for a few miles, he suddenly answered the question I'd put to him at the lunch counter.

"So you want to know why they don't let me play in the gambling capital of the world? It's because they know I'm gonna rob them. Walk right out with their money, and they gotta just stand there and watch me."

"And how do you do that?"

"With these," Boris said, lifting his hands from the wheel for inspection. "With these mashed-up beauties I make cards and dice do weird, wonderful things. Do you understand what I'm tellin' you?"

"So you cheat."

"My friend," Boris answered, after weighing my statement with a few nods of meditation, "there was a time when I would have objected to that word. I would have put in a claim that I was an artist, or a Robin Hood who only stole from those who wanted to steal from me. But now I accept the word 'cheat.' Boris Blake at your service, the best dice and card mechanic in the world. No more, certainly no less."

"How good can you be if everyone knows your profession?" I asked. It was a question that made Boris wince.

"I've been at this for twenty years," he said in his best

injured tone. "All over the world I've busted out games that no one thought could be taken. I've spotted cards with cream cheese in poker sessions in the Catskills and switched in shapes right under the nose of the toughest greaseballs in Brooklyn. I mean I took their money, friend. Right out of their goddamn pockets. I . . . took . . . their . . . money! Hell, once when I was in jail I threw in a cooler against four Muslims in one game. I had no fear, that's why I was the best."

Suddenly Boris turned off the highway and headed up a side road that seemed to lead nowhere.

"But now, I've just been around too much. Even though no one's caught me in the act, there's just too much suspicion, too much heavy heat. I can't even do a little light work now and then without someone starting a beef. Fame has been thrust upon me, and I can't do anything about it."

"Why don't you retire?" I asked. "You must have made enough by now."

"Young man—after that remark I get to call you 'young man'—what the hell is enough? Come on, you're a gambler, you tell me what's your limit."

It was a good question, one which I had always known I would have to answer.

Suddenly Boris stopped. There was nothing around us for miles, which is exactly what he seemed to want as he scanned the area. When we got out of the car, we were almost knocked down by the desert heat, and for a minute both of us were afraid to breathe or speak. Slowly, I began to slide back into the air-conditioned wagon.

"No!" Boris finally gasped. "You've got to get out. I can't show you anything in there."

"We'll get a stroke if we stand out in the sun," I said, and tried to close the door past the wedge Boris had made with his body against it.

"Just ten minutes. I'll show you my work in ten minutes.

Everything that I can teach, but enough for you to walk away with that whole goddamn town over there."

I looked at where Boris was pointing and saw, shimmering in the heat, a Las Vegas of vague, liquid colors and undulate forms.

Boris opened the rear door, took out a folding table, and set it on the hard, baked ground. Then he brought forth a small trunk, which he placed under the table, and two folding chairs. He asked me to sit in one, then took a deck of cards from the trunk and began shuffling them.

"You can understand," he said while performing neat, tight riffles with the deck, "why I wouldn't want to display all this in a hotel room. One nosy bellboy who tells a few stories and all those crazy cowboys who think they've gotta kill somebody once a week got me with the goods. Then they just don't ask me to leave, they do a little job on my body while I'm going."

Boris set the cards down on the table and motioned to me to cut them. Then he began his performance, speaking only to explain the precise nature of each manipulation or to exhort me to look closely at his large, mangled hands. For a few minutes, in that cooked wasteland, I watched him work his magic. Bottoms, seconds, annulment cuts, deck switches, holdouts, palmings, waving—all were displayed in swirls of easy movement that made a mockery of the senses. The demonstration ended with my dealing him hands of blackjack which he converted each time into the jack of clubs and ace of diamonds.

"Well, what do you think?" Boris asked, sweeping the cards from the table in a quick, single-handed movement.

"An impressive display," I said.

"Only part of my repertoire," he beamed. He then returned to the car and, from under a tarpaulin, removed what looked like a small, topless coffin and placed it on the table. When I peered into it, I saw that it was a scaled-down craps table, correct in every detail, even to its sides being covered by tiny rubber spikes to insure that dice would carom in a manner that can't be predetermined. Boris knelt down at one end of the long box, rolled a pair of ruby-colored dice along the length of the shooting surface, and asked me to examine them. I counted the number of spots on each side, made sure they were cubes, and let the sun flash through them to reveal any impurities.

"All right, toss them back, if you think they're legitimate."

I did, Boris picked them up, rattled them for several seconds, and then sent them crashing against my end of the table. When they came to rest, I saw that their color was now a deep emerald, and on closer inspection I discovered that the dotted sides contained only three numbers instead of six, that there was no possibility of their forming a combination that totaled seven. They could therefore be rolled forever and always make the shooter's point.

"How's that for a switch?" Boris asked.

"Magical," I answered.

"No, just work motivated by a love of larceny. Of course I don't switch in a pair of shapes like that except when I'm playing with some retards."

He then produced the red dice from a hollow in his hand that had been covered by a lump of muscle at the base of the thumb.

"All right," he said, "now I'm going to hold up a six, five times in a row. Keep your eyes on the little red squares."

Dizzy from the sun, I struggled to focus on the dice as they careened and bounced about the table. As Boris predicted, one of them always came to rest with a six-spotted side upward. Boris said nothing after the rolls were over, as if he divined my thoughts and had no wish to interrupt speculation on what it would mean to master such an art.

As we drove back to Las Vegas, Boris still avoided the subject of my becoming his pupil. Instead he told me about the event that had started his decline as a mechanic.

"I mean I had done real well for over fifteen years. Movin' from Miami to Vegas, from San Juan to London—anywhere there was action. And I never had no heat. I mean any time I wanted to I could drop into a joint and pick up five or ten. large and slip away like a thief, like I'm Boris the Invisible. Then I go to Greece 'cause I hear they've opened up some new casinos there, and it figures that the joints oughtta be pretty soft, with dealers who don't even know how to count chips yet. Well, I walk into this place outside of Athens, a beautiful, plush layout with a view of some ruins up on a hill, and it looks just like a piece of cake. The dealers can't even peek at a hand without flashing their hole card and the guys at the dice table, half the time, forget to pick up a losing bet. I mean I could have played on the upsky and beaten that joint *all* the money. But I gotta do what I've taught myself to do, right? Which meant a little holding out at the blackjack table. Nothing too strong. Maybe three times an hour I come in with a twenty-one from my pocket, and nobody even thinks of blinking when I do. I'm not lookin' to make an impression, so after I've won about two thou I tip the dealer real nice and head for the cash-in window, thinking it's all been sweet and easy, and that maybe I'll drop back in a few days and hit for the same number. Then, just as I'm being paid off, this guy in a uniform walks up to me. He tells me he's Captain something-or-other and points to a nameplate and a badge he's got pinned on his uniform. Right away I know there's gonna be a beef and that the best way to handle that is to come on strong, start shouting about how much money you've dropped in their joint. how they've got some nerve to get nasty when you finally have a little run of luck, and in general make them want to get you out of there before you start scaring away all their customers. But for some reason I don't want to get this guy angry. It was hard to figure what he was gonna do. I mean, for Chrissake, how do you take a reading on a guy with triangles in his name. So, *schmuck* that I am, I let him take me back into his office, where we are joined by two sullen gorillas, also wearing badges and a lot of geometry on their chests, and I resign myself to getting bruised or giving back the money. However, the Captain offers me a chair and starts chatting with me real nice, asking me if I'm enjoying my stay in Athens and why I'd chosen Greece for a vacation. I answer him soft and polite, and for a minute I think maybe he's just some guy from the tourist bureau assigned to find out what kind of clientele the casino's attracting. Then he goes and opens the window and he stares at whatever you call those ruins at the top of the hill and very softly he asks me, 'Mr. Blake, why do you cheat?' just like that. Like he was asking what hotel I was stayin' at. Well, I say, 'I beg your pardon?' and he, with his back still to me, he sort of sighs and says again, 'Mr. Blake, I would like to know very much why you cheat.' Well, I'm forced to make a little protest at this you understand, so I give him my offended act and start to get up from the chair. This stirs up the gorillas, however, and so I sit down, and very calmly demand an apology. But he just turns around, smiles, and asks me the same question again. Did he see me cheat? I ask. Did anybody see me do anything wrong? He shrugs and wags his head like it didn't matter if anyone actually saw me making a move or two, like all he had to do was stare at my ears to tell that I'm a swindler. Then he starts a spiel about how cheating is really no more than robbery, and when you rob you make society a little worse than it was, and since you're part of society you've made yourself also a little worse. Now, I'm listening to this—with two grand of the joint's money in my pocket, I feel I can afford to listen even if the guy is coming on like a mental case—and nodding like it's makin' sense. So he goes on and on, tellin' me that by palming an ace in his joint I'm really holdin' out on myself since I'm swindling what I'm a part of and no sane man is gonna do that, right? Right. But I say to him that I, Boris Blake, was robbing nobody. Only passing a little time. He shakes his head at this, like he's more disappointed than steamed up over the way I stick to my story. Then he picks up this little broken statue that's on his desk, you know one of those goddesses with drapery on them that you find in every junk shop in Athens. He gives it to me and asks me to look at it. It's about a foot high and real heavy, and as I'm running it down, thinking the lady's shoulders are a little broad for my taste, the Captain tells me who the goddess was and what she was supposed to have done and all sorts of things like he was a museum guide. Then suddenly right out he asks me if I think she's beautiful. Of course, I give him what I think he wants to hear, and tell him yes. He takes the statue back, nods at it—I'm getting an uneasy feeling that the guy is pure crazy by now—and then he asks me what I would think if I saw somebody relievin' himself on this beautiful statue. I start to laugh, but I gulp it right down when I see how serious the Captain's face is. I tell him it would be terrible, and he says, yes, it would be terrible because it would show ignorance. I go along with that, and then he makes a quick mental move back to me robbin' the joint. I'm ignorant of what I'm really doin', because I don't understand it. How can I understand what I didn't do? I shoot back at him. But if I had done it, would I understand it? And if I didn't do it, would it matter, if I didn't understand what I didn't do? I mean that was his ploy. Every time I answer a question, he's got another one, and I feel like a job's being done on me, but I can't figure where the con is. I just keep answerin' yes and no, no and yes, until I don't know what I'm talking about. I mean all I can get is that this guy is tryin' to prove that I'm some kind of moron or a thief, and I'm not buyin' either one of them. But it's like I'm standing on two chairs that are being pulled further and further apart. Finally I say no when I should have said yes or vice versa. He gives me a nice big smile and says, 'So, you did cheat us, Mr. Blake.' I give it one more shot at sayin' no, but he goes over everything we've said, all the questions and answers which to him, and to the two gorillas, prove that not only am I a bandit, but I'm a dumb bandit as well. Then he sort of pats my shoulder and says that you can't blame ignorance too much, so if I'll just return the money there'll be no official action taken. I figure okay, it's a standoff, so let's be civilized about it. I take out the cash and put it on the desk. This guy looks at it for a while and then he shoots a little sly look at the gorillas and suddenly each one grabs onto an arm so that my hands are stretched out flat on the desk. And this Greek bastard sort of shrugs, and brings that square-shouldered lady down on my left hand, then on my right, and then twice more on each of them. I won't even try to tell you what the pain was like. I mean I just kept whimpering all the time they dragged me off to some doctor, who doesn't do nothing but wrap some bandages around them so the bleeding doesn't show, and then to the airport where my bags are waiting for me along with a ticket out of the country. Then the Captain has my picture taken just in case, even with the banged-up hands he's given me, I come up with some way to beat the gambling joints, because, as he says, still talking soft and reasonable, it's hard to learn to be an honest man, even when you've really had a good teacher. Every casino in the world is gonna get a copy of my picture just in case I get confused about things again. Then he puts the statue next to me on the waiting bench and walks off."

When we stopped in front of my hotel, Boris told me that I didn't have to make my mind up right away. Then he held his hands out in front of me.

"In one year I had them working again. But the pictures ruined me. And to tell the truth, I never could've really made it in class joints. I got a bad face. I mean it's pretty easy to read me for larceny. But you, no one could ever take you for an outright weasel. You could bring what I know into places that don't let me through the door."

I told Boris that I would let him know my decision, but I really considered his proposal to teach me his craft no more than a fairy-tale boon, like a cloak of invisibility or a golden touch. It had its fantastic appeal, but I was still confident that I needed no wiles in order to gamble successfully, that I would naturally find my way to good fortune.

However, during the next few days, this confidence in myself began to fade. As my money dwindled, anxious swells passed over me, cold intimations of failure and permanent dishevelment, of a lifetime spent in a casino mob that scurries pointlessly from promise to promise. I kept demanding to win, but could still not find the courage needed to make winning possible, and so I went on changing games and tables, betting five or ten dollars at a time, waiting for an impossible run of luck that would, in an unbroken string of right choices, retrieve all the thousands I'd lost.

During this time, Boris did not talk to me again, but everywhere I gambled, he made a brief, pointed appearance. As a defense against immediate ejection, he had taken to wearing ridiculous disguises—beards, wigs and glasses, behind which it was absurdly easy to recognize his condemned features and detect his soul's devotion to chicanery. We of course didn't acknowledge each other, and I would continue gambling as though I'd never considered making a pact between us.

One morning, at about five o'clock, I believed my luck had finally changed. All night I had been losing, and I now had nothing left of the money I'd brought to Las Vegas except two thousand-dollar traveler's checks. The evening's long series of defeats had left me too exhausted to go through the procedure of cashing one, a process that had naturally become more difficult as my appearance deteriorated, and I began a slow retreat from the casino's center tables. On the way, I stopped for a second at all the slot machines, hoping to find one that had been left primed by an absent-minded player. This was indeed a low ritual, indulged in by the most debased victims of bad luck who milled about the downtown casinos. But for the last few nights, I had tried the handles without shame, unembarrassed even when I knew I was being contemptuously watched by employees and players alike.

Somewhere in the middle of a row of dollar machines, I drew down a handle and felt it slip past the locking gears. I took a breath, continued to pull, and indeed the machine sprang to life, its strips of colored symbols humming into a single blur that, after three separate clicking stops, would resolve into a trio of bells, fruit and golden bars.

However, when the whirring stopped, it was not these usual symbols I saw in front of me. Instead, one, then another, and then a third small red heart appeared behind the glass covering, and before I could check its diagram of winning combinations, the machine began to buzz, brighten and pulsate with colored lights. I rushed to snatch a cup from a nearby table just as a long metallic retch was followed by a clanging spew of silver dollars from the mouth of the machine. I filled the cup, my pockets and my hands, and still the flood continued, coins dropping around me on the floor, adding their clatter to the noise the machine still made to advertise its generosity. Other players stopped to help me retrieve them, and even those who had been uneasily entertained by the sight of my attempting to coax free chances from the slots, joined in the search and brought me, with congratulations, my silver dollars.

When all had been found, a guard escorted me to a change booth, where a smiling lady presented me with a large, round pin that had the casino's name and "Jackpot Winner" stamped on it. Then she counted my coins and changed them into a form I could more conveniently carry—a single hundred-dollar bill.

Naturally, it was not the amount, but the way of obtaining it, that made me feel certain I'd been given the sign I'd waited for during the weeks of slow, grinding descent. I sensed I was again part of a formal drama that was constructed from the beginning with a just resolution in view. Not to act decisively after such *ex machina* intercession would mean that one should forfeit the right to gamble forever, and, so, wearing my winner's badge, with the vision of three tiny red hearts held in my mind for triple courage, I went to the craps table, and bet the hundred dollars when the dice were passed to me.

I lost on the first roll, which caused no stir among the stickmen and players at the table, but which took me several horrible minutes to comprehend. And even when I understood that an event had indeed just taken place that put an end to dramatics, I could not accept that I'd been used with such cruelty. I had not expected gambling to create for me a world of honorable coherence, but neither had I expected a malicious one. To have tricked me with a false sign, a sign that no one who nostalgically wishes for meanings in things would not trust in and follow, meant that gambling was as perverse as any of the old philosophies I'd abandoned; that it was no more than raw and raucous data. I watched the dice bounce upon the table, the chips and money pass back and forth between those who ran the game and those who played in it, and rage began to swell inside me. Never had I been so toyed with, so beguiled by apparent meaning, and when I was calm enough to leave the table, I'd decided to accept everything Boris had offered me.

For the next hour I searched for him in the casinos and all-night bars along the streets and avenues of lower Las Vegas. By now it was well into morning, but there were no social signs around me of a day's beginning. Instead, I saw all the activities of night perpetuating themselves, and the people caught up in them, whether just wakened or driven past sleep by fear or amusement, appeared unconcerned with ordinary notions of time. They were used to conducting life's business according to schedules of private noons and midnights, and they filled bars at eight in the morning as comfortably as they did supermarkets at eleven at night.

Instead of the unease I usually felt when I found myself drifting from one day into another without the traditional pause for sleep and ablutions, I enjoyed the disordered morning. The mixture of di- and nocturnal attitudes helped strengthen my resolve to give up all desire for a design to life, and as I'd freed myself in Munich from an addiction to pure thought, so I now was ready, in lower Las Vegas, to abandon my gambler's superstitions.

Since it was proving difficult to find a disguised Boris among the early-morning rabble, I decided to let him seek me, certain that it would not take very long before he sensed my readiness to come to terms. To make his search easier, I entered a casino I played in often, and walked slowly and conspicuously about the tables, distinctly remembering how I'd lost at almost all of them. I could even discern my old auras at the chairs I'd sat in; sad, unkempt penumbras of energy that faded a little with each losing bet. All that expense of spirit, I thought, for nothing; all that care and calculation wasted.

As I moved toward the room's entrance, my way was suddenly blocked by a file of tourists behind a guide who announced he was leading them to one of Las Vegas' most famous sights. I waited as they passed, and then watched them form an adoring crescent around the promised wonder—a large glass rectangular case that held, in cash, a total of one million dollars.

"Here, ladies and gentlemen," the guard droned in a voice struggling with early morning phlegm, "is probably your first and last sight of one million United States dollars."

The tourists made appreciative noises, and then quickly fell into mute reverence, transfixed by the sight of neat rows of ten-thousand-dollar bills seemingly suspended in the air. Some moved their lips in silent counting; others blinked and wagged their heads in a manner that suggested a desire to disbelieve what they were seeing, as though they wished there were no reality to the number they so often invoked whenever they defined a perfect life. A boy, whose attention wandered for a moment to the pistol worn by the display's guard, had his head firmly turned by his mother until he again directly faced the goal she was quietly setting for him. A young man and woman, who were dressed in a way that revealed they'd come directly from one of the town's twenty-four-hour wedding chapels, clasped each other around the waist, as if to reassure themselves that love doesn't need so much common currency, and that the life they'd planned was still a wonderful ambition.

Finally the guide decided it was time to dissolve the solemn mood that had settled over his tour. Clearing his throat for attention, he began in a quiet, soothing voice to tell a joke about a Texas millionaire who kept his rolls of hundred-dollar bills in his bathroom to be used as toilet paper. When asked why, the Texan had answered: "If somethin' don't cost a hundred dollars, it's no fun doin' it." There were sputters of laughter, enough at least to break the million-dollar spell. Then after the guide further amused them by smothering the glass-covered money with passionate kisses, they went away content to have put another item on the tour behind them, one which, several were bold enough to say, had proved, after all, a little disappointing.

I, however, was impressed, for I knew if I accepted Boris' tutelage, I would have a seven-figured answer to the question, "How much is enough?" If my fate were now to be reckoned in numbers, then one million would be a proper premium for my having learned that there was nothing more to life than the counting of its parts, the gathering of bits and pieces of experience which, in sufficient number, can deaden the mind's passion for a systematic world. The money before me meant an easeful passing of time. If it was not enough to blot out seizures of fright in the manner of an emperor, to divert myself with games, grottoes and executions, it was sufficient for a comfortable retirement. Looking deeply into the glass of the million-dollar display, I could even see the garden in which I would cultivate my resignation, a place of fountains and cypresses, of shade mixed with meridional sunlight, of bleached gravel paths and sloping terraces, a setting designed for wry thought and doleful memories. I looked again and saw the villa I would own, and, in its one unshuttered window, myself looking exactly as I did in reflected superimposition on the rows of ten-thousand-dollar bills. I wore pajamas, a soft straw hat, and a look that expressed no interest in keeping up appearances.

But then this picture of genteel seclusion faded, and only the money remained. The cold thought struck me that in order to acquire the necessary real estate for my retirement I was going to have to go to work. There would be no single moment of revenge in which, masked in innocence, I pillaged the halls of gambling. Rather, there would be long hours of modest thefts, days and days of pleasureless travel, months, perhaps years, of slow, disciplined cheating that would cause no suspicion. Work was the only description for the wage-earner's time I saw stretched before me, for the long sessions of rudimentary exercises I'd have to master before my hands could perform the most simple devious maneuvers. After a life of dramatic reflection, I was accepting the fact that my purpose lay in the learning of a trade, that I must labor in order to achieve nothing more than a comfortable old age.

This, however, would be the price for that certainty that was lacking in the symbols of logic and slot machines. Once a few mechanical skills had been mastered, everything would be inevitable, and I could shape my fortune like a careful potter. Only an immature mind would balk at the boredom in this order of things or feel shame over the manual labor involved.

But whether immature or nobly childlike, my mind did reject this outline of the future. Aching with fatigue, it still managed to rouse itself into remembrance of old duties and imperatives that had no reason for being except that they were mine and formed the private definition of myself.

I turned from the case of treasury notes, and went to the

cashier's window. I pushed one of my thousand-dollar traveler's checks and a passport toward two suspicious clerks. They scrutinized me carefully and studied my signature and photographs. Finally, I was verified to their satisfaction and the money was counted and delivered to me.

I took a seat at the roulette table, made a small bet on the even numbers, and spun my mind with the wheel. The cycles of thought whirled into a single argument against the small strategies of life that promise certain compensation. But to refute certainty requires a logic that finally turns its sting upon itself, and dies gasping "There is no greatest number," or that " 'How much is enough?' is a meaningless question." And yet if a man wishes to excuse a life lived at random, then he must first exhaust all of philosophy in order to justify idly waiting for a pleasant surprise or a graceful windfall. And when there's nothing left of thought, then must there be silence? Not in the least. We simply return to the beginning, to the alternative that was always present in the lighter Platonic moments. Which is to say, we make up marvelous stories about ourselves.

When I returned to my hotel, I found my luggage had been moved to the lobby. In my abstracted state, I'd not paid the rent for the last two days, an oversight that had caused my eviction. The dour young bellboy who had welcomed me was at the desk, and he informed me as I paid him that my room was now occupied. Then in a tone that both offered advice and anticipated its refusal, he mentioned that a bus stopped at the hotel in a few minutes that went all the way to San Diego for less than twenty dollars. What he could see, I already knew; Las Vegas and I had worn each other out.

The bus, filled with tired Las Vegas refugees, was just about to leave when, from my window, I saw Boris waving at

175

me frantically. He was in a padded cowboy suit, and wore a henna-colored wig and a short matching beard. With an exaggerated fat man's waddle, he moved alongside the bus until I shook my head several times in emphatic refusal. He stopped then and threw up his arms in a gesture of bafflement. I waved to him and thought how simple it is to resist temptation when submission entails a greater effort.

Chapter VIII

It was the diamond I saw first, a streak of white light that flashed by my eye like a comet. I had been playing poker for nearly three days, excluding eight-hour respites for sleep, and when not in a hand, I had learned to rest my eyes by letting them gaze down on the green felt of the table and look for patterns in the stains and cigarette burns that earlier players had left. I would raise my head only when an odd vibration in the rhythm of play called for scrutiny of the faces of those hunched about the table, faces that, like the blots and smudges on the table covering, often transpired hidden designs to an imaginative eye.

The diamond, however, startled me into alertness. I watched the small, pale hand that wore it work with its companion in a deft shuffle of the cards, a smooth, rapid mixing that made the large jewel's brightness trace shimmering lines in the air, as if the hands meant to bind the deck they held in ribbons of light. Without waiting for the cards to be dealt, I leaned back in my chair and observed the dealer.

She was as pale as the precious stone she wore; yet it was a paleness that betrayed no fragility. As it matched the diamond's hue, so it seemed also to share its hardness, its mineral durability, and the features of her face were perfectly cut facets, fine shadings that betrayed no flaws or feelings beneath their glowing whiteness. In this sculptured light there was, as in the stone itself, a delicate blue suffusion, and the eyes that caused this subtle coloration were exquisitely empty, their beauty that of immaculate design and pure function. Her hair was flaxen, short, brushed back like a boy's, as if to keep its softness from flourishing. She sat erect and perfectly contained in her chair, a concentration of cold purity upon a throne, an avernal queen.

Gardena is a town sprinkled about a web of California highways. By day, one might pass by all of its landmarks—gas stations, motels, supermarkets, churches, schools—and not realize that anything truly communal existed within its city limits. All the flaking white-framed houses, all the gaudy stucco of fresh suburban architecture, would seem, at noon, at a speed of sixty miles an hour, no more than a brief diversion, a blur that becomes lost in a traveler's memory among billboards, drive-ins, diners, markets, car lots and other weatherworn roadside structures.

And at night, Gardena has even less substance; for it is then no more than slivers of neon among the beads of light that mournfully mark the roads and thruways, making darkness and distance more forbidding than they would otherwise be were there no tiny white points by which to measure them.

After Las Vegas, I had sought a place of spiritual and

financial discipline. From what I had heard of Gardena, it satisfied both needs. Although it is a town famous for gambling, the gambling is not that of great sums and pure chance. The only game officially allowed within its city limits is poker, and then only those forms that can be considered variants of draw. Years ago, when morality caught up with western expansion, a group of California legislators made playing poker illegal in public. However, through honest oversight, tendentious omission, or simple ignorance, only the term "stud poker" was incorporated into the statute, a loophole which the councilmen of Gardena took advantage of to create a local industry. Gradually, Gardena became the host to those in search of everything from a night's diversion to a way of life. To accommodate these desires, the town sanctioned the construction of several large card emporiums, poker palaces that, with their restaurants and TV lounges, are the true public buildings of the community. The playing areas are marked off by brass rails or wood partitions, against which lean the recently impoverished, the casual spectator, and the player waiting for a place to be open at the table and game of his choice. In contrast to a casino, there is hardly any sound; almost, considering the amount of people present, a disconcerting stillness. Occasionally a cry of protest or a moan of disappointment becomes distinct, but these soon die away, consumed by the soft, steady drone of ritualized card-playing.

And the playing is, indeed, almost all an exactly established ritual. To keep personal tragedy at a minimum, or at least to diffuse its impact and publicity, rules and wagering limits have been devised by the overseers of Gardena poker so that it is nearly impossible for one hand to be flamboyantly decisive in a customer's life. There is a maximum amount that can be bet before the draw, and a similar limit, generally twice that of the first, that can be made afterwards. There are no restrictions on the number of raises two or more players may engage in, but only drunkards or those with very strong hands indeed make honest use of this option. Generally, this concession to gambling's need for infinite possibility is taken advantage of by a pair of veteran players in order to flay an unsuspecting tourist; that is, they will continue to raise each other so that no matter how often the outsider calls, he will be faced with one more commitment. Even the most ingenuous visitor will soon understand the trap he has fallen into. Sometimes he will protest, but since he is a stranger and those who have whipsawed him are regular customers, the official he pleads before will do nothing but listen sympathetically, comforting him now and then with homilies on the inherent risks of the game he is playing.

So much then for the financial discipline I sought. As for the spiritual, it was present from the minute I entered my motel room, a cubicle rich in all the details my mind thought up whenever it wished to furnish a setting for loneliness. A chair, chest-of-drawers, an end table, all chipped and peeling, utilitarian items that were meant to serve unnoticed, but that had been painted or varnished to provide a touch of gentility for their temporary owners. On one wall a mirror, the paint from its frame spotting the reflection it cast; beside it, a large print, a seascape, gray, with forlorn waves, its sense of space as closed and confining as the room it was in. On the floor, like a squashed poodle, a scatter rug relieved the linoleum monotony that surrounded it; behind a brown canvas screen, were a stove and refrigerator, sad, forlorn, domestic things, absurdly out of place. A television set, a double bed that vibrated when a quarter was put in the slot attached to the headboard, a single window with plain cotton curtains translucent enough to filter the light from passing cars into the room—these completed the furnishings.

Often I had told myself that I could live alone in such a place, that shabbiness and solitude were an endurable fate. If one purposely lives by gambling, then such mournful rooms are always a possible terminus for an unlucky life. Still, whenever I imagined myself in such quarters, I shored up my spirit in the same way I did against all ideas of a dull eternity. My mind would sustain me, memory and wit transforming a rundown room, as they would vacuous eons, into a habitable space.

The reality, however, had proved grimmer than I'd imagined. I'd been in the room just long enough to unpack, deposit the required quarter, and stretch out on the quivering bed when I began to see precisely the unmanageable horror in such emptiness and disconnection. The images that came to me in the darkness were those of a life lived without ornament or diversion, of an existence conscious of nothing but its own ending. By the time the bed had finished rocking me, I knew that I'd been a braggart in the past whenever I'd told myself that anything was supportable if it was the result of my having gambled on an extraordinary life. In less than half an hour of Gardena motel time, I came to know how much I would miss the gossip and diversions of the world, and so I took out a pack of cards and began dealing myself hands of poker, preparing for the games I would have to play in order to earn a first-class passage to anywhere far from this place.

"Parmi les morts, il faut de la patience," a Haitian poker player named Beausourire had once told me. He had been speaking of Gardena's steady clientele, the men and women who everyday take the same seats and play the same game, hollow spirits who knit or munch sandwiches while folding hand after hand, waiting for someone rash enough to bet on two small pair or to think that a flush will stand up to the demands of three raises. Beausourire was one of the best card players I had ever known, someone who could break a game of prodigal Harlem pimps with a single hand, but who could also subject tight, percentage-playing professionals to the slow torture of his insights and calculations. He had played everywhere poker was known, and his stories of wins and occasional losses had always been colored with common sense and good humor. Only when he had spoken about the play in Gardena had he reverted to what I supposed was his native view of the world.

"It is not poker that one plays there. In a game of poker, I can put the players' souls in my pocket. But in that place, there is nothing. Time marches along, the cards fall, someone coughs, someone scratches the head, someone now and then might even curse. But don't be fooled. All these are just imitations of living things made by those who have no spirit at all in them."

I had asked Beausourire why he had gone to Gardena in the first place, and why he hadn't taken an early leave once he'd found it inhospitable to his gambling style. We were sitting at a sidewalk table of an Eastside restaurant in New York, and before he answered, he looked at all the early-evening life streaming past us, the white Rolls-Royce he had left double-parked, the thin, gold Patek Philippe watch that peeked out from beneath the cuff of his white mink jacket, and at the small silver snuffbox he had converted into a container for the cocaine he used when the length of a card session demanded it. Finally, he took in the face of the girl who was sharing a bit of his life, and who was now peacefully drawing through a straw the foamy remains of a Brandy Alexander. He looked at each of these with careful appreciation, and then answered:

"My man, you don't go to Gardena, you end up there. And it's not easy to get out, because the dead love company. They don't let go easily."

In New York, caught up in the energy of a metropolitan dinner hour, I had found Beausourire's description fanciful. However, my arrival at the motel had shown me that the Haitian's narrative was more objective than I had thought, and when I stepped into the Red Horseshoe, the poker parlor whose lights I could see from my motel window, and took my seat at a ten-and-twenty-dollar table, I began to suspect that his description of place and people, far from being embellished with Haitian fancy, was rather the understatement of a gambling realist.

A tall, frail lady of sixty, who wore rimless jet-black sunglasses, whose silver hair was arranged in tight little curls, whose hands, delicate reticulations of bone and vein, manipulated, it seemed simultaneously, the mound of knitting held in her lap and the cards she dealt out or received; her partner, a small, plump, intense woman of the same age, whose eyes followed every move at the table with unabashed mistrust, whose dark face, lined and dappled from the sun, brooded over the cards she cupped in her hands so that not a speck of pasteboard was revealed; a toothless but erect Japanese, a man beyond the ordinary meaning of human age, who emitted soft sounds of mental distress no matter what cards came to him and who demanded that one understand that a sigh meant he was raising, a whine meant a call, and a dry cough signified a checked hand—these were the regulars at my table when I sat down for my first day of play. Immediately, since mine was a new and lively face, the women began to work in collusion, raising and reraising every time I stayed past the draw. I let them win a few small antes, and then ended their ploy by raising both of them, standing pat, and then raising again after the draw.

When they folded, I felt a silent communication pass between them, a resigned agreement to beat me with better cards rather than with tired card-parlor maneuvers.

But they did not succeed any better playing honestly, nor did the cacophonous Japanese. They left, and others tried their skills and routines against me. But I was not beguiled, and in three days' time, I had won close to two thousand dollars, a considerable enough sum considering the house limit and the betting habits of the *moribundi* against whom I played.

The reason I won was not that I was a significantly better player than those I was matched against. I am good at poker, but I am not one of the game's elect, and those who came and went at my table could estimate the probability of a hand's success as rapidly as I and take the action proper to the situation, which is all a good poker player who lacks sublime intuition can do. My success was simply the result of my being ready to gamble on hands about which neither mathematics nor psychology provides a reasonable basis for decision. It was at such moments that my opponents, for whom even a sizable advantage was worth only the smallest risk, were most vulnerable. Their minds were filled with too many memories of strong cards being beaten by innocent fools who took every raise before the draw, and they were therefore ready to fold at the faintest sign of danger. They were good poker players, but they had played too long, endured too many debilitating turns of luck, to be truly threatening, so it was a simple matter to take advantage of their lack of spirit and force them to accept small losses whenever a sanguine character was required to see a hand through.

The wearer of the diamond, however, I found, after an hour's play, to be a much subtler opponent. She was not one who thought that poker had been created to nourish the virtue of patience, and she was as ready to do battle with the unknown as she was with the obvious scapegraces who wandered in and out of our game. Her style was never routine, and she emanated a force of will that was absent in the other players, a fierce, pressing involvement that would have made her tactics seem frantic had they not contained such strength and calculation.

As the game progressed, it became a contest between the two of us. Again and again we drove other players from the pot and won or lost to each other in a precise, alternating sequence. She would turn over a flush to the king and beat mine, which stretched no farther than the jack; I would counter by topping aces-and-jacks with a low three-of-a-kind. But the best moments were those in which we maneuvered and probed each other, standing pat with nothing, bluffing on a one-card draw, or even breaking a pat full house in order to coax a bet after the draw. Each gambit was like a flirtatious exchange, in which neither of us gave any outward signs of communication or enjoyment. What was taking place was a secret recognition of affinity; we courted without expression and with a cold courtesy.

Then came the moment that brought the coquetry to an end. I was dealt a pat hand and bet. Those to my left began to fold, but then I saw the diamonded hand reach for a stack of chips and put in a sum that indicated a raise. I looked up from my cards and studied the raiser's face, knowing that it would betray nothing, but wanting to seize the opportunity to stare shamelessly at its severe beauty. I prolonged the moment for as long as possible, and then I raised her back.

For the first time since she joined the table, she hesitated, and then, as though her thoughts were elsewhere, she nodded, matched my raise, raised again, and tossed two cards away. I counted the chips that had been added to the

pot, and then turned to the dealer. Protocol demanded
that he should be the one to state that an irregularity had
taken place; that, since I had been raised, no cards should
have been discarded before giving me an opportunity to call
or raise in return. However, he said nothing, indeed seemed
startled that I should turn to him for assistance. The other
members of the game were also silent, their expressions indicating no interest at all in the outcome of a hand they were
not involved in.

"Excuse me," I said, addressing the dealer. "I believe I
have the right to call and raise."

The dealer, an old man who affected western dress and
mannerisms, smiled thinly and pushed the filthy cowboy hat
he wore down over his eyes.

"You want to see and raise the little lady?" he drawled.

I looked at my cards and again saw the low straight that
had been dealt me. Not the strongest hand in the world, but
it beat anything that could use a two-card augmentation. I
nodded.

"Then go right on and do it," the dealer said.

I did.

Suddenly she spoke, her tone sharp and injured.

"If that's the way you want to take advantage of a mistake, I'll call your raise and raise you again."

Now I knew something was afoot. Even if she were capable of making a mistake that revealed the nature of her
hand, she would never whine about it or compound the error with a spiteful bet. Although I should have increased
the pot again, I merely called and signaled the dealer that I
needed no further cards.

"I don't need any either, I guess," she said softly, and
returned the two feigned discards to her hand. "And if you
bet, I'll have to raise again."

It was a low, obvious trick, but it had worked. If her

hand was what it seemed, my straight would lose ignominiously. And if she was bluffing, if she thought me astute enough not to try to guess the level of her deviousness, she was right. I folded my cards and left the table.

I was at the short-order counter of the restaurant when she came up to me and apologized.

"I figured you knew everything except the oldest trick in the house," she said. "And it was time to leave anyway."

"That's all right. I learned something."

She took the stool next to mine and looked up at the menu on the wall. The crisp delicacy of her features again impressed me; she seemed fashioned from a formula that distilled human perfection, a formula never meant to be personified, that omitted all the imperfect details and accidents of mortal flesh. More and more she and her diamond blended in my mind, and when she touched my hand, I was surprised to find that her fingers were soft, and that their warmth revealed a human temperature.

"You've been doing very well here," she said, and smiled a little, her fingers still resting on my hand.

"The competition wasn't too hard until tonight."

"Yeah, you've made these old players cash a lot of retirement checks. But they do all right in the end. They beat the tourists, break even with each other, and lose to me. But their plots are all paid for, and I leave them enough to be comfortable till they're dropped in them."

"That's charitable of you," I said, a supercilious remark that I immediately wanted to retract. However, my companion took it as an honest compliment, and declined it by confessing it was to her interest to keep her sources of income alive for as long as possible. Then, as though she were testing my character as she had at the card table, she added, "There's nothing good about me at all."

I thought a moment, wondering whether to take exception to this statement or to laugh at it. Instead, I simply replied that I believed her. She smiled, and ordered a glass of milk and a cheese sandwich.

While she ate, she told me that her name was Daisy and that she had first come to Gardena three years ago on her honeymoon.

"You're married?" I asked, never having considered she could be part of any life except her own.

"Not any more. He died. A week after we left Gardena—where by the way he lost three hundred, he couldn't play at all—we went to Mexico. By that time, we'd been married about two weeks, and I'd decided that I'd had enough of him. Especially when he began spending the money I'd won here on funny sombreros and ugly Indian pots. I wanted to come back to Gardena with a stake to play poker on—so I killed him."

The last remark was washed down with a long drink of milk. An emphatic pause followed, which I did not intrude upon. Since I didn't care if she'd murdered her husband, there was no reason to feign shock or to make her insist on my credence.

"How did you do that?" I asked.

"We were in Durango, walking through the market in some little town, when suddenly he started to shake, sweat, and grow pale. I asked him what was wrong, and he pointed down at the counter we were standing in front of. You know what was on that counter? Ashtrays with scorpions in them covered by glass. The scorpions were dead, but that didn't make any difference to him. He was terrified of them. Scorpions must be the big tourist attraction in that part of Mexico because each one of the ashtrays had 'Recuerdo de Durango' written on it, which means 'Souvenir from Durango.' My husband, however, was one tourist who was not

188

attracted. He went straight back to his room, announced that we were going home the next day, and went to bed. I could tell he wasn't much of a man the way he played poker, but this really made me sick. I was going to walk out on him, but it occurred to me that a wife who leaves her husband after two weeks wouldn't get too much alimony. So I decided to go for the insurance policy."

She insisted that she pay when she finished her sandwich, and as we were walking out asked me where I was staying. When I gave the name of my motel, she said she was certain I would have picked that one. When I asked why, she told me, with a trace of disappointment that I hadn't guessed, that it was where she lived. She had been there for nearly three years.

"Aren't you interested how I did it?" she asked as we began our way back to the motel.

"Did what?" I was pondering the three years spent in the drab confinement of our Gardena motel.

"Killed my husband. You know what I did? While he was asleep, I went back to the market, bought fifty of those ashtrays and broke each of them open. I put dead scorpions all over the bed while he was asleep and still had about two dozen left to scatter around the floor. Then I waited until morning, went out, and knocked on the door. From what he had shown me at the poker table, I took the chance that he didn't have the strongest heart in the world. It was a good guess. I heard him go through his wake-up mumbles and coughs, and then there came something like a squeak and a long whoosh of air followed by a thud. I tiptoed back into the room, made sure he was really dead, collected up the scorpions, flushed them down the toilet, and the bride got away with a perfect crime."

"Honeymoon heart attack," I said in the darkness, and

smiled at the thought that Daisy, for all her lucidity at the card table, might very well be mad. Even to imagine murdering a man with souvenir scorpions hints at a maniac's brain, and I wondered, when she invited me into her room, how much I was prepared to risk in order to make love to her.

But I followed her through the door without hesitation. We were in a room that was almost a replica of my own. A bowl of flowers had been added, there were a few more kitchen utensils, and an extra mirror hung on the wall. Apart from these, there were no other signs of a three-year residence. When she opened the closet, I counted two dresses and two pair of dark gray pants, exactly like the ones she was wearing. When, with her back to me, she took off her sweater, she put it into a drawer that contained almost nothing else. From the hook on the bathroom door, the usual resting place for slips, nightgowns, pajamas and showercaps, she removed the only item hanging there, a short terrycloth robe, and put it on. From one of its pockets she took a deck of cards and began dealing five hands of poker to herself, each of which she played with fierce concentration. I watched her and wondered if I had been invited into her sparse chamber for anything more than fresh combat at cards. I thought, perhaps, that it might be the only way she could make love, that enticement and submission for her had no meaning if they were not joined to the symbols of the game she had mastered.

However, when she completed the hands, she put the cards away and sat quietly, her legs folded, on the edge of the bed.

"I was telling my fortune," she said softly.

"Those were poker hands you were dealing."

"I have my own way of telling what's going to happen

to me with a deck of cards," she said, beginning to unfasten her robe.

"And am I going to happen to you?" I asked, watching her body reveal itself, thinking that there was something almost ominous about its formal, lucent beauty.

"I guess you are," she said calmly, continuing to undress until she wore nothing but her diamond.

That night I was sensually enchanted. With pinch, caress, tender and obscene phrase, Daisy led me past the boundaries of pain and pleasure, into a state of such furious delight that I felt myself free of any distinctions of mind and body. Thought became an instant erotic attitude, an enfleshed fact; and breast, thigh and orifice were the clear wit and logic of the world. And whenever this unity was weakened through emission, Daisy would, with her diamond, magically restore it, sliding the stone gently along my spine until I was roused again past any need for mortal rest.

It was not until morning that she let me sleep. When I awoke, I was drained and anxious, uncertain where I was or whom I was with. Daisy was sitting in a chair, thumbing through a magazine and occasionally jotting down something in a notebook she balanced on her knees. She was naked, her body caught in a little shaft of sunlight, and I marveled at how even a practical morning view could not diminish her beauty, could not reveal even a shadow of weariness beneath her eyes or a line made by heavy sleep.

She was aware of my staring at her. Without looking up from her reading, she asked if I wanted coffee, and with this offer I knew that I was back in ordinary space and time.

"Did you believe what I told you about my husband?" she asked, her back to me while she fussed with cups and saucers. I was following the contours of her body, trying to find some touch of asymmetry, some reassuring imperfection, and answered that it hadn't mattered whether she'd made up her scorpions.

"That's good," she said, "because I can't stand people who care whether stories are true or not."

"They're like poker players who want to know if you were bluffing after you make them fold," I said.

She was pleased at this, and kissed me when she brought the coffee.

"Speaking of stories," I said, looking pointedly around the room, "have you really lived here for three years?"

"It doesn't look it, does it? You might guess I arrived here the same day you did. You know why that is?"

She didn't let me begin the answer I was starting, and it was just as well, for she might have taken offense at how lightly I treated the lack of human clutter around us.

"It's because I don't have any things," she said gravely. "But I'm going to. Just as soon as I've made the amount of money at poker that I've set for myself."

"How much is that?"

"At first it was a hundred thousand dollars. But the list of things I want keeps growing, so now I've pushed it up to two hundred and fifty thousand. But . . . that . . . is . . . it. That should buy enough things."

She invested the word "things" when she spoke with deep, wistful feeling, as though it conveyed the most precise ambition, the most vivid purpose of life. When I didn't seem to understand her enthusiasm, she went to the chair and came back with the notebook she'd been writing in.

"I've got it all down in here," she said gravely. "With the place to write to and the price. When the time comes, I won't have to waste any time shopping around. Look it over. See if you think I've missed anything."

While she showered, I sipped coffee and glanced through the notebook. There must have been over a thousand entries, a catalog of modern material wants that began with "Rancho Colonial House #32, $46,000, Sunfun Enterprises, 187 Willit Boulevard, Santa Barbara, California," and ended with "Colored Polynesian Sponges (6), $5.95, Oddsort Importers, Box 405, San Francisco." In between were items of furniture, ornaments for the house, clothes, kitchen supplies, a station wagon, a camping tent, and a radio that was advertised powerful enough to receive messages from ships at any point on any ocean of the world. Things that came in boxes, bottles or shipping crates; things that would arrive with the manufacturer's promise that they would always share your life; and things that were meant for no more than a moment's use—all were listed apparently in the sequence in which they'd come to Daisy's mind. When I tried to imagine them all together, all brought into the service of a single being, I saw nothing except great pyramids of trash with Daisy sitting satisfied and naked on top of them.

"See anything I've left out?" she asked, sending a shiver of lust through me as she dried her body with a worn-out motel towel.

"Do you really want all this?" I asked.

"Of course. Why else do you think I play cards every day?"

"I thought you loved poker."

Daisy frowned at this and delivered an important precept. "I don't love anything about it. That's why I'm so good at it. I don't need it for any reason except to get all the things I've written down in my book. That's why I always win. That's why I can beat all those tight old ladies. I have a goal. I'm not going to sit here turning cards forever without a reason."

She stopped and pointed to the notebook.
"And it's all in there."

That afternoon, and every afternoon for a month, Daisy and I went to play poker. We entered the clubs together and then took seats in different games so that we wouldn't be forced to combat each other or be suspected by the other players of collusion. We would play almost until closing time, receive receipts for our winnings, and then go back to the motel where I would be turned into pure appetite for as long as I could hold back sleep.

Between poker and love, there were stories, wonderfully matter-of-fact accounts of crimes and mayhem. At first, only Daisy narrated, but after a few days she let me understand that I was also expected to create a life for her entertainment, one that equaled the biography of wicked deeds she'd revealed to me. And so, on alternating nights, we scotched, dispatched and ridiculed a good deal of the world's population in our tales, trying to outdo each other in the number and heinousness of our acts. If she claimed that as a child she had locked a claustrophobic aunt in a broom closet, I would counter with the precocious assault on an enfeebled grandmother. She told of seducing, at the age of eleven, her English teacher, a sad, repressed pedophile who hanged himself immediately after changing her grade from F to A. I recounted how a young ballerina, when I demanded that she jeté through a window four stories aboveground to prove she loved me, had done so with pirouettes of joy as a prologue to the leap that would leave her crippled forever, and how, when soon after I told her I was leaving, she asked only that I always keep her tattered ballet slippers as a memento of our love.

On and on we went in this way, never smiling, never with

a playful look or skeptical expression. I had no idea what
her tales meant to Daisy, or what sort of facts lay behind
them. It was easier simply to accept the life they made up,
to believe that we were both unfeeling predators, preternatural wills that responded only to their own kind.

Each day I awoke to find Daisy adding to her list of things.
From the catalogs and magazines that made up her only
mail, she would carefully select an advertised item or two
for inclusion in that future moment when money orders
would be sent around the world to claim the personal spoils
poker had won for her. It was at these times that I would
glance anxiously at the calendar on the wall and force myself to count the number of days that I'd passed in Gardena,
to recall that I had set out to win and enjoy the entire world
as a gambler. While Daisy attended to the coffee, I would
resolve to leave, to return to my room, pack, and, without
even waiting to cash the receipts from my latest winnings,
depart by the first means of available flight. But then Daisy,
as if sensing this resolution, would come toward the bed, offering her body like a potion, to be sipped or drained in a
single gulp; and the world I would go to faded away, and I
owned no ambition that she could not satisfy.

I had, of course, read many stories of such enchainment,
but I had never before believed them. The conqueror who
gives up honor and empire to lie for a night in his lady's
arms, the lovers who damn their souls for their bodies' sakes,
the wan poet's agony over empty-headed beauty—such situations I had always felt belonged to the mythology of human feeling, to the need to dramatize desire, to infuse it
with the overblown attributes of destiny. In the sensual
world I'd known, I had found no such compelling embodi-
ments of passion, no incarnate beauty so fateful that it could
have disfigured my life. Like most of my contemporaries, I
went from body to body as need demanded, a disinter-

ested sensualist, an abstracted, self-preoccupied lover. I was certain that it was impossible to reach those heights, or depths, of physical enthrallment that brought ruin to noble natures. There could be no one in the world like Daisy, no one whose physical beauty could shadow my life so that I could no longer see its clear and distinct purpose.

But time passed, and I stayed on. I became the fettered consort to the woman who ruled over the poker palaces of Gardena, a position which darkened the good opinion I had of myself, but which was curiously honored by her withered subjects. Wherever I sat to play, they treated me now with a special deference, offering to include me in their conspiracies against an unwary tourist, even, I believe, at times propitiating me with small bets on hands they suspected were lost.

Attempts were also made to be social, to draw me into the gossip and doings of their grim fraternity. One evening, during a break in play, the man who'd dealt that fateful hand I'd lost to Daisy, tipped his stained hat to me as I passed his table in the restaurant and asked that I join him.

"How you doin' today?" he inquired, after insisting on buying me a steak like the one he had in front of him, which he prodded from time to time with his fork but never tasted. "You run into any fat ones?"

"It's been pretty slow," I said, wondering if such a thin, reedy throat was capable of swallowing a solid piece of meat.

"It'll liven up, son," he said and winked. "I hear part of the fleet's come into San Diego. That means we should be gettin' a lot of sailor boys down here over the weekend. You can squeeze a lot of juice from them."

"Is poker all that attracts them to Gardena?" I asked. "Isn't there a whorehouse or two around where they can at least get a little pleasure for their money?"

The old cowboy stiffened.

"We don't have nothin' like that in Gardena," he said, his voice rattling with prim satisfaction. "And that's a funny question for you to be askin'."

"Why's that?"

My companion shrugged, and rasped out a little burst of laughter.

"Well, seein' as how you got yourself the finest lookin' lady in town. Not to mention its best poker player."

"She's beautiful," I said. "But she uses some low tricks at the table."

"You're talkin' about what she did to you? That was just savin' time. She was gonna win anyway, even though you handle cards as good as anyone who's—just passin' through Gardena?"

There was a slight taunt in the way his remark ended in a question, but I let it go and asked the cowboy why, if Daisy always won, he and all the other regular customers still played with her.

" 'Cause it's an honor to have her around," he said, as if this were a fact that shouldn't have to be explained.

At this point we were joined by two old women who were in bitter dispute over a hand one of them had lost the previous night, and the conversation became what it would usually be during such interludes. Someone would recount an entire evening's poker session, card by card, while the rest sighed and commented on how hard it was getting to squeeze a profit from the game. Ailments then came next, bladders and arteries matched against spells of vertigo and constipation. Finally, the rising price of those pills and elixirs that sustained them and how one had best pass away quickly before a decent death became too expensive. It was the tired, empty banter of the aged, except that when anyone mentioned an event from the past, or the doings of their children, there would be a silence, as if something ill-mannered had been said, and the speaker would hurriedly bring the conversation back to a subject that Gardena contained, a subject that would not spill over into memory or conjure up images of extraneous life.

"It's your turn to tell a story," Daisy said. I was undressing her, a privilege only recently granted me and which I was in no mood to dilute with Grand Guignol narratives.

"You've heard all my stories," I said, drawing her sweater over her raised arms and admiring the abrupt, pert appearance of her breasts.

"No, I haven't," she said, stepping back, her arms folded across her chest. "Tell me something terrible you did."

The way she had withdrawn and covered herself angered me just long enough so that I began a story unlike any I had told her.

"All right, Daisy. Once when I was a student in New York I got very drunk and went off to find a girl I knew who was always happy to see me no matter what time of day or night I appeared. She lived in a huge old apartment building on upper Broadway that had been converted into a place of a thousand cheap rooms—cubicles for students, addicts, prostitutes and anyone else in need of a cheap place to sleep, by the hour or the year. The inside of the building had been chopped and twisted into a maze of corridors, partitions and stairs that often led nowhere. To cram as many people in as possible, floors had been put up between the old landings of the building, so that the numbers on the doors meant nothing, and many of the rooms had only a curtain drawn in front of them for privacy.

"As I said, I was drunk, and I couldn't find the room the girl was in. I walked and walked, listening at doors, hearing groans, coughs and arguments, and sometimes a scream or very soft weeping. I passed people in the hallway, but they had no idea who the girl was I was looking for or where I could find her if they did. Finally, I gave up, and started down a flight of stairs I thought would lead to the building's lobby. Instead, they ended abruptly in front of a door, which I supposed led to another corridor or landing. And so I opened it.

"You know what was behind the door? A room with a cot, a sink, and maybe a chair or two. And standing in front of the sink, right under a bright hanging lightbulb, was a naked man, very old, with skin shriveled and wrinkled past anything I'd imagined age could do. He was washing clothes in the sink and hanging them to dry on a clothes-line that sagged from the ceiling. He had a ragged piece of wash in his hand when I burst in, and he clutched it to him as though he thought I meant to steal it.

"I started to apologize, but then I saw something horrifying and remarkable. The old man sported an erection, a huge, ugly, rigid erection that rose out of all that wrinkled skin as though it had nothing to do with the body it was attached to. I couldn't believe there was still such desire in someone so old, and I kept staring at the smooth, inflamed flesh until the man modestly covered it with the tattered bit of laundry he'd been holding in his hands."

"What did you do to him?" Daisy asked impatiently.

"Nothing. I was terrified. I ran back up the stairs and down a mile of corridors until I found a way out of the building."

"What kind of story is that?" Daisy said sharply, folding her arms more tightly about her.

"It's a true story, Daisy. One that came back to me the first night I was in Gardena."

"It doesn't make any sense to me," Daisy said.

"I'm sorry. It does to me."

"I want another story," Daisy said flatly.

I looked at her and knew that, whoever she was, no honest

tale I could tell about my world would interest her, even if she could understand it. And yet, for my own sake, I felt I must try.

"No more tales of horror, Daisy. I'm beginning to be offended by them. I'm a man of some literary taste, you may be surprised to discover, and the tales we tell each other are cheap, gory little dreams that make the world look despicable."

Daisy remained a sullen blankness, so I spoke more bluntly.

"I'm a gambler, Daisy. And there's nothing in Gardena to gamble on."

Her expression indicated she understood this, but did not approve.

"Come with me," I said. "I'll teach you everything I know, and we'll share everything I'm going to win."

"How do you know you're going to win?" Daisy asked, and since I had no answer she added: "And I don't have to be taught anything."

"Don't you want something more than to be the Poker Queen of Gardena?"

"Everything I want, I've written down. And it's all going to be sent to me here, all the things I've won because I can beat anyone who comes to Gardena with poker on his mind."

"You'll never win enough," I said. "You'll never catch up with your list."

"I'll know when to quit."

"Good poker players know when to quit," I admitted. "But only after they've known what it is to lose. You're always going to win, and you'll go on forever, until you've filled a thousand notebooks."

Daisy didn't understand this image of empty infinity. She seemed puzzled, almost hurt by what it implied.

"Do you want me to tell you who I really am?" she said shyly. Amazed at this offer, I answered that I did, and I prayed to be surprised and touched.

"When I am sure," she said, suddenly again herself, "absolutely sure you're never going to leave. Then I'll stop all the stories and we'll tell each other our real secrets."

She unfolded her arms and stood so that I could finish the disrobing. As I peeled the garments from her, I thought that Daisy was right, that since I would leave, since I must leave, there was no point in any homely truth between us. And when she was naked, a nacreous smoothness in the motel room, and still insisting on a story she approved of, I told her how, motivated by boredom, I once assassinated a powerful minister of state and thereby sent half the world to war for my personal amusement.

Sometime after that night, I stopped playing poker. I grew tired of winning, every day, half as much as Daisy did. The game had become nothing but empty labor, a usurpation of the strength I needed for the love Daisy and I made at night. And so, each day after she left, I would spend the afternoons strolling about Gardena, trying to make the time pass quickly with visits to drugstores and supermarkets, followed by explorations down quiet residential streets that were meagerly shaded by a few weary-looking palms. I stared over hedges and fences at houses that aped the style of Spanish castles, Tudor manors and Texas ranches. Occasionally, I would glimpse someone entering or leaving, and hear the sound of a door closing. More often there would be no signs of life except lawn sprinklers slowly rotating in the afternoon sun, sending up spirals of fine spray that settled without luxuriant effect on the amber lawns that invariably surrounded a small rose and cactus garden.

It was on such a walk that I crossed one of the many

highways that pass through Gardena, and came upon a great expanse of razed earth and huge excavations, acres of land in the process of being developed into a new Gardena neighborhood. Although there was nothing that resembled streets, signs had been planted in the ground that told you that the mound of rubbish you were now walking on was to be called La Paz Boulevard, and that what looked like a giant shell crater would bear the name Beechwood Drive. One house had been built, a model for those that were to come, and stood, flowing with pennants, on a hillock of rock and ferrous clay. A billboard was beside it, telling its price and name. It was the house Daisy had entered in her notebook, Rancho Colonial #32.

Some days, however, I would not go out at all. I would stay in bed, have food delivered to me, and take frequent naps, thin snatches of sleep that allowed me a certain control over my dreams. In them I walked along elegant boulevards or across warm tropical beaches; marvelous buildings appeared, bright, chatter-filled restaurants opened their doors to me; schooners carried me into a deep azure distance. And there were sometimes rococo rooms to pass through, places of candelabras, girandoles, frescoed ceilings, and long, soft, sad conversations that, through delicate inflection and nuance, passed a civilized judgment on life.

As the afternoon went on, I managed these dreams less and less effectively. Landscapes and figures grew menacing; cold winds blew through chambers empty now of all company. In another form, Daisy would appear, fiercely erotic no matter how I disguised her. I would awake then, restive and tumescent, and wait for her to come home. And this last hour or so was passed, as I had as a child passed periods of punishment, by watching the clock relentlessly shorten a span of useless time.

The day I discovered that items were being entered in Daisy's ledger that were meant for my future use, I knew I must flee. The list of things—among which were a battery-operated Japanese razor, straw house slippers, and the Sears, Roebuck Complete Gentleman's Den—read like an indictment. Terrified, I flung the "Book of Things to Be" against the wall, dressed, and went to the bank to withdraw the money I had put there. Then, still full of resolution, muttering to myself the catalog of monstrosities that Daisy had destined for me, I returned to the motel and earnestly began to pack. But then, among the clothes we had mingled when I moved into her room, I came upon that bit of small white raiment that was always the last item to be slipped from Daisy's body when I undressed her at night. I stared at this token of the feeling that prevailed between us, and I couldn't help touching it, squeezing the triangle of slick nylon in my hands, rubbing it across my cheeks, forehead and lips. Before I put it down, all resolve to leave had been drained from me, and I faced the fact that I might be alone with my passion forever.

I first heard of the man's arrival when I was summoned at about midnight to the motel office and told there was a telephone call for me. This in itself was odd, and for a minute I was afraid someone I had once known would be on the line, someone from my past who would demand explanations for what I was doing with my life. But it was only the old cowboy, who told me in a brisk, dry voice that Daisy was involved in what appeared would be a long session at the poker table with a film producer named Dorian Goldman, and that I shouldn't expect her home at the usual time.

I went back to my room to wait, but I'd become someone

too addicted to precise sequence not to feel panic at this postponement of the pleasure I'd waited for all day. I found this need for Daisy's body despicable, but when she was not home after a two-hour, fretful wait, I abjectly went out to find her.

It was nearly closing time when I entered the Red Horseshoe, and most of the tables were empty. Nevertheless, there was more noise in the room than I had ever heard before, heavy, good-natured bellowing that was completely unlike the groans and bitter whisperings that rose out of the usual stillness. In the far corner of the room, one table was full, and a number of spectators stood around it. As I approached, I glimpsed Daisy, controlled and lovely, in the process of studying her cards. On either side of her were two ladies, more thin and thanatoid than any I had seen before, staring blankly in front of them, obviously capable of adding nothing to the game except their frail presences and the illusion that it was not a one-to-one confrontation that was taking place between Daisy and Dorian Goldman. Two men, who looked as though they might be the women's mates, sat on either side of the film producer.

And it was he who was filling the huge room with his voice, booming out a monologue that, sustained by frequent sips from a silver flask he drew from his coat pocket, celebrated himself and his achievements. He was a heavy man, but not fat, with shoulders that began just beneath his ears. His face was round and tanned, with large, black, melancholy eyes. What hair he had left, he combed shamelessly forward, so that the top of his brown head was covered with tiny, slick, serpentine curls. He wore a blue pin-stripe business suit that was barely able to contain his bulk, a white shirt and silver tie, both of which had been spotted by the contents of the flask.

"Again I say it, this is the only way to relax. Who wants to lie in the sun when you can turn a few cards and see how your luck's running? What the hell, gimme one card and I'll see if I can hit this straight right in the belly."

I caught Daisy's eye as one of the old women dealt Goldman what he had requested. Composed and immaculate, she took one card and bet without comment. Goldman glanced at his cards, then tossed them away with a shrug.

"Well, maybe it's too early in the game to fill inside straights. Still, I feel like I should get any card I want. Everything else in my life is coming around. In one year, two ex-wives who've been bleeding me dry up and get married, one to a Spanish faggot, and the other to a golf pro. Both of them broke as I was going to be if those two ladies hadn't gotten off my back."

He drained his flask, then slipped it with a twenty-dollar bill to one of the floormen, who, since drinking was officially forbidden in the game room, discreetly retired to earn his tip. Then Goldman looked admiringly at Daisy.

"You're really serious about this game, aren't you?" he asked, and then laughed at his own question. "Why shouldn't you be? Everyone is serious about something. That is, everyone except my son who told me, after I went into six figures to get him a Ph.D., that he's too smart to take anything seriously."

Goldman had folded his last two hands before betting, and Daisy, in order to keep the game from seeming too dependent upon his willingness to play any cards dealt to him, went through a shallow routine of winning and losing a small pot to the old ladies at the table. From the amount of chips she had in front of her, she was winning well over a thousand dollars, all of it I assumed from Goldman. The last entry in my column of the ledger had been an Italian-made electric typewriter that cost $932.00, and I shuddered at how quickly Daisy was erecting in my honor a tomb of merchandise.

But she was too engrossed in her sack of Dorian Goldman to notice this reaction. After his brief pause from play that followed the introduction of his son into his chatter, the producer was in three large pots and lost them all. He chastised himself during and after the play of each of these hands, recalling how he had once worked nearly a year in order to earn the sum of money he'd just thrown away on the last batch of feeble cards.

"And the asses I had to kiss to raise the money for my movie! But it'll be worth it. Because about this film people are going to say 'honest,' 'artistic,' 'inventive,' 'opulent,' 'hilarious,' 'tragic,' and, goddamnit, 'entertaining.' It might even get a few of you away from the poker table to see it."

Since play was being held up while new stacks of chips were being delivered, someone in a bored voice asked the name of the film. Goldman smiled, and his eyes opened as if to take in the magnificence of the vision evoked by his picture's title.

"*The Man Who Bought the Roman Empire,*" he said. The response was all silence and blank faces.

"*The Man Who Bought the Roman Empire,*" he said again, as if repeating the punchline of a joke that hadn't gone over. "One hundred dollars says no one here knows who that was."

"Didius Julianus," I said, as if dropping the name of an old friend.

Daisy frowned at my intrusion, but Goldman looked at me admiringly.

"What do you do, hustle history?" he asked as he handed me the hundred-dollar bill.

"He's a famous man," I said. "Every schoolboy used to learn the 'Rime of the Roman Emperors.' 'Though just and good, old Pertinax/ From the praetors got the ax/ Then a fortune Julianus pays/ For a reign of sixty days!' "

"My God," exclaimed Goldman, who had, in fascination, been nodding his head to the beat of the doggerel I'd spouted. "That's worth another hundred if you write all that down for me."

Daisy riffled the cards to interrupt us, and, a new batch of chips in front of him, Goldman nodded that he was ready to play. However, before looking at his cards, he gazed back at me with half-drunk penetration and asked if I thought he had a good subject for a motion picture in Didius Julianus. The tone of the question had to it the need for an authority to pronounce the dream of Dorian Goldman a sound investment; and by virtue of my knowledge of the "Rime of the Roman Emperors," I assured him that he had a dynamic subject for the screen, one that should provide deep truths, in a suitably entertaining form, about the wonder of mortal ambition.

"I'll buy that," Goldman shouted, slamming a bet down in the center of the table. "Mortal ambition. Yes, I have had mortal ambition. It made me produce films about professors that turned into insects, housewives that became cannibals, and things from outer space that took over the bodies of a major league baseball team. And I'll tell you something, I was never ashamed of my monsters. They were right up there, just a little behind *Dracula* and *Frankenstein*."

Goldman laughed, and then called a raise Daisy had made. She showed three sevens.

"What do you know?" he cried, fanning his cards out smoothly in front of him. "I made a full house and didn't even know it I was talking so much."

It was the first hand I had seen Goldman win. Daisy glanced quickly at me, and her eyes flashed a pointed accusation. I was making things too comfortable for Goldman, too easily diverting, with the result that he was betting blindly, without recourse to the simple-minded wiles and strategies of the poker tourist. The effect was no usable information for Daisy, and I was being ordered to retire, to await my dole of pleasure in our motel room while Goldman was dispatched in the proper manner.

I took one retreating step from the table, but then stopped. Aware what I was risking, I nevertheless gave Daisy just the hint of a defiant smile and asked Goldman how he had ever thought of making a movie about the man who had bought the Roman Empire.

"Destiny," Goldman roared, after a long swallow from his flask. "I had reached that point in life when I either had to go on thinking up bigger and better bugs or do something that showed that Dorian Goldman gave a damn how he lived and died while he was here. I had just about made up my mind to stick with the bugs, when my son tells me that I remind him of this Julianus fellow with all my talk about doing a really big picture, that it was like I wanted to buy an empire for myself. So I do a little research, and I find out that this Julianus really did pick up the whole damned ancient world at an auction. Ordinarily I bet a flush, even if it means I'll have to walk home, but this time I fold without a fight."

Goldman turned up five clubs, and from the abrupt way Daisy tilted her head, I gathered that she'd held a better hand and had counted on a nice-sized coup should Goldman have anything as strong as a flush. Again she looked at me, displaying the full force of her beauty, the sum of what I stood to lose if, by staying, I became Goldman's ally against her. It was a clear warning, and I might have heeded it had I not seen something odd about her face, something that helped me to defy her and continue to encourage Goldman's enthusiasm and absent-minded luck. I pulled a chair up to the table and asked if I might try a sample from the flask.

"Help yourself," Goldman said. "Anybody else want some, be my guest."

I took a long swallow, the first drink I'd had since arriving in Gardena. The heat and aroma of good bourbon enveloped me, and I graciously offered Goldman's flask around the table. There was a long pause, and then one of the old ladies, whining softly about a pain in her hip, fluttered her hand toward the flask. It shot back into her lap when Daisy snapped the cards and asked if they were going to continue the game.

"Of course," Goldman said. "I've just started getting lucky in this place."

As one of the old men dealt, I took another long drink from the flask while I studied Daisy's face. I had been right. Beneath her eyes were two crescents of shadow, two bits of moon-shaped darkness so faint that they would have been noticed by no one who had not scanned and memorized every millimeter of her body. "What did you find out about Julianus?" I asked Goldman, placing the flask on the table between us. "I don't remember much about him except that he was an ambitious senator."

"Forget senators," he said, flashing me his hand to show that he had just raised one of the old ladies on a pair of eights. "There's no drama in a guy who's been important and rich all his life taking a shot at being emperor of the world. No, I told the screenwriters I hired that I wanted a self-made man, someone who starts off with nothing and works his way up in life until he thinks that the only thing left for him to do is own the world."

"Definitely an improvement," I said, as Goldman easily bluffed the old lady from the pot with his two eights and a bet made in mid-sentence.

"For fifteen million, I get to create my own history," Goldman laughed. "So we have Julianus starting off real low in the world, hustling slaves in the provinces. He does all right, but then he gets an idea to start putting on some sex spectacles, and he soon starts catering expensive flesh shows for private parties in Rome. You can imagine what scenes that will make on the wide screen. I mean can you believe a girl and a bull going at it in front of a mixed company of fifty people eating dessert? But it's historically accurate, so no one can start a legal hassle about it."

The rest of the table had been made uneasy. The men shook their heads, the women squirmed, and the old cowboy, who stood behind Daisy's chair, began a little tremble of rage. I felt that they might shatter under the impact of Dorian Goldman's creative energy, especially since he had just won a good-sized pot with a broken straight and a series of offhand bets. Daisy had not stirred, either at the mention of catered orgies or at the ending of the hand. But the shadows had darkened a little and there was just the trace, perhaps, of two thin lines at the corners of her mouth. Not enough, I thought, to liberate me, even with the transfusion of ambition that I was receiving from Goldman, who had bought the man who bought the Roman Empire. But if he could keep winning, if he could sustain in me the excitement of high gambles, then Daisy's spell might be broken long enough for me to flee through a crack in her perfection.

I drank again from the flask, and asked Goldman how he had been able to film the copulation of girl and bull.

"That's a secret between me, the special effects department and the girl's agent. But don't think the film is nothing but left-handed sex. Politics, greed, love—it's all in there, especially when Juli starts rising in society, buying the hills of Rome one by one, acquiring exclusive rights to the aqueduct, putting up a temple in the best part of town to honor his mother's memory. He knows that he's despised by the bluebloods, but he keeps on flaunting his way with money at them, making them all come to him for loans and advice. He's so confident that gold can do everything, that he even, in his prayers, offers Apollo a million in cash to rent the sun for a day."

"What does he want to do with the sun?" I asked, closing my eyes as Goldman drew three cards to a pair of jacks after enduring a quartet of raises. When I opened them, I saw a third eight and two fours had arrived.

"Aha," Goldman exclaimed, raising his flask high in salutation. "I asked my writer the same question, and he tells me its because Juli wants to transcend, whatever that means. I'll call and raise."

He won the hand, and the flask was refilled. He was now flushed and asweat with motion-picture dreams and the near-flawless hands of poker he was being dealt. As he trusted the transcendence of Julianus, so he was now all confidence in his cards' good fortune, and he often bet without looking at those that came to him after the draw. As he talked of himself and his Roman hero, I began to feel again the strength of human audacity, the excitement of desires that were not meant for simple satisfaction. I now looked at Daisy with cruel, restless eyes. I saw her face begin to crack like crystal, the incisions of age zigzagging through flesh that grew loose and heavy, dragging her features down into distortion. Thin, knotted veins appeared at her temples, which the strings of wild gray hair failed to cover. With a ravaging sight, I destroyed the passion that had hobbled me, forcing Daisy into successive portraits of decay, until the diamond was the only radiance left her. Like all men who outgrow a particular enthrallment with bone and flesh, I had excuses for what I did to Daisy in my mind. She had been, after all, a cold seductress, a form of death, an enemy of manly virtue. She deserved all the deadly signs I laid upon her. And even after she began to beat Goldman, to win hand after hand while he rambled on about the execution of Julianus and a final freeze-frame shot of a severed head staring sightless at that sun which could not be bought for a day, Daisy's spell stayed broken. The beauty that returned with her gain of Goldman's final chip, I had at last made powerless.

It was nearly noon when the game ended, and Goldman, worn out and beaten, got shakily to his feet and complimented Daisy. He'd had luck with him for a long while he said, but he had been careless. However, he assured us, with his movies he had not been, each frame of which he had brooded over for months.

He agreed affably when I asked him to drive me to Los Angeles, asking only that I try to come up with a sequel to the Julianus story on the way. Though she listened to us, Daisy did not look up from the careful stacking of her chips. I imagined that at that very moment she was beginning a story about me, a revengeful tale of pain and punishment. I left her to her dark inventions, and walked with Goldman out of the room.

While he waited in the car, I packed in minutes, and gave no last look at the motel bed for memory's sake. I did, however, once we were on the road, turn to gaze back at Gardena. But it was not a town to recede slowly in the distance; it had simply dissolved.

Chapter IX

The large oval window of the Marco Polo suite looked directly out on the harbor of Hong Kong. Junks, sampans, ferries, steamers and warships speckled the darkness with lights that blended on the window glass with the reflections of the softly lit lamps behind me in my room. In the center of this small firmament, glowing like a thin corposant, was my own reflection. This superimposition of myself dressed in a white linen suit against a background of shimmering strings of lights, was a picture I had composed each evening for over a month.

I had not come to Hong Kong straight from Gardena. Exhausted by my escape from Daisy and her inventory of worldly goods, I began in a desultory way to gamble again. In ugly, mythless towns like Reno and Elko, Nevada, I played for small stakes, waiting to recapture a sense of excitement at the tables. However, whether I won or lost, I continued to feel stale and sluggish. Soon the casinos I frequented began to look alike, and the brief at-table friendships with other gamblers became a barren routine. Except for an occasional sad imitation of Daisy, I spent long, womanless hours in my rooms, watching television or reading the Gideon Bibles I found tucked in the drawers of night tables. Sometimes, there would be passages underlined by previous readers, and I spent hours trying to imagine what sort of person it had been who had found an urgent cogency in a law of Leviticus or a metaphor of Isaiah.

Then one morning I woke up with a clear idea of what I had to do. No dream or line of Scripture prompted me, only my old desire for the adventure of movement. I realized I had the whole world in which to gamble, and in that world there were places more open than the Nevada desert to the making of fortunes. Moreover, the further I went from the safety and comfort of familiar things, the more meaning gambling would have now, for should I be assaulted and neatly wiped out by bad luck, I might never have the chance to return to old surroundings and reclaim my past.

I bought a map of the world and, spreading it out on the floor of my room, sat down and scanned the cartographer's markings for a continent to invade. I dismissed Europe as too full of cultural and personal memories; Africa as too inhospitable at that moment to Western gamblers; South America seemed to me a place for commonplace destinies; and Australia was no more enticing than the Arctic poles. That left Asia, and I circled Hong Kong as my place of entry.

After deciding on my destination, I tallied up my resources. I had neither won nor lost in great amounts since leaving Gardena, but there had been a slow, dribbling attrition that had reduced the sum I left Gardena with by some five thousand dollars. Still, when I added my cash and traveler's checks together. I had more than twenty thousand dollars left. Enough to lay a respectable seige to fortune in a far-off place, for I planned to take my total wealth with me.

I added the dash of full commitment to my fate by buying a one-way air ticket. The night before I was to leave, I packed slowly and deliberately, excited again by how simple it was to transport one's self and valuables through the world. Then, when everything was nicely stored and ready for travel, I sat down to write notes to a few friends and the woman I'd lived with in New York. I tried to frame their good faces in my mind as I explained what I was about to do, but the lineaments would not hold, and what expressions they formed no longer had an immediate connection to my life. In the morning, I decided to destroy the letters I had written.

On my way to the airport, I thought of all the emissaries and exiles my culture had dispatched or hounded to the part of the world I would soon be in, men who drifted across strange, mapless geographies in search of more impressive destinies than they had left at home. These pale, restless foreigners, tuans and outcasts, despised and deified, founders and despoilers of kingdoms, had left stories behind them that I felt were antecedents of my own.

Later, during the long flight across the Pacific, my feet in paper slippers and my body wrapped in a silk kimono provided by the airline that carried me, I grew more sober. I admitted that recent history had softened the firm opposition of East and West, and that the once dark hostility between the two worlds had become, through wars, commerce and universal politics, an enlightened enmity. Still, I felt I would at least soon be in a place whose history and mine enjoyed little common ground. I would be farther from my past than I had ever been before, and there would be no language, landscape or architecture to remind me too often that greater journeys had been made before mine.

My first days and nights in Hong Kong were spent in simple explorations. Stepping out of the lobby of my hotel, I entered the hot, fumy dampness of the city and set out to absorb the strangeness around me, to reassure myself of the distance now between me and everything recognizable.

Content to be lost after a few twisting blocks, I strolled through streets filled with garbage, merchandise, and the vibrant noise of commerce; streets that were tunnels of banners and wall posters, labyrinths of gruesome caricatures and Chinese calligraphy; streets that ran through sunny parks, around empty pagodas, and past quiet, walled-in gardens. I browsed in cluttered shops where only the keenest eye could pick out the precious object from mounds of cheap trinkets. Merchants eyed me like hungry lizards, and offered pearls, jade, celadon and ivory; carved boxes, belly-swollen Buddhas and dragon figurines were plucked from crowded shelves and displayed for my naïve inspection; spices and aphrodisiacs were extolled in suggestive whispers; scrolls, skulls, shrunken heads, Malacca canes and sinuous Malaysian krises were praised for their magic and rarity; vases that claimed Sung, Ming and lesser dynasties as their provenances were held up delicately in the darker corners of shops while their owners demanded prices that probed the foreigner's ignorance and resources.

I bought nothing; I simply looked and walked on. Now moving along the harbor, past the quays covered with stalls filled with shrimp and rotting melons, I watched the water families fish at one end of their boats and defecate at the other. Then past the blank stares of old men and street urchins, I went deeper into the city, resting for a moment against the iron fence that surrounded a green and immaculate cricket field; then going on until I turned to catch what breeze there was coming from the water and watch the ships steam in or out of port, certain of their destination.

216

I paused in these wanderings only when the air grew too stifling, and my clothes too sodden, for me to go any farther. Then I sought refuge and refreshment in the nearest bar. Remote from American and European pathways, I usually had only Chinese ideograms to guide me, and I would stare dumbly at these graceful, hermetic markings, feeling curiously elated at being free for a time from the harassments of language.

When I found, through luck or directions, a suitable place, I would slouch in, order something cool and alcoholic, and sit alone, waiting to be revived by the fan-cooled air. No one disturbed me; indeed, these bars were generally dim, deserted places, tabernacles for old men who sipped quietly from bowls of rice wine or glasses of warm beer. Most of the conversations I heard around me were in whispered Chinese, soothing lullabies of sound that helped slacken the race of strange new images that ran through my mind.

One afternoon, after being replenished in this way, I found myself, a little drunk and lightheaded, in a large square where a rally of young Communists was being held. Almost all those present were Chinese, and, dressed in the loose-fitting blue uniforms of mainland Maoist fashion, they stood at respectful attention while they were enlightened by a succession of speakers who addressed them from an impromptu platform decorated with ferocious portraits of Marxist leaders.

One of these speakers, however, was European. He was a thin, middle-aged Englishman, dressed in a rumpled gray suit and holding, as if it were a shield, a large briefcase in front of him. He spoke in a weary, low, nasal voice, his words stretched out and stuttered as he crouched a little to project them directly into the microphone that stood in front of him. He was there, he drawled, to speak of unity, and to assure the audience that, in the West, there was a rising sense of conscience, a spreading feeling of sympathy with the great social experiment being carried out by the Chinese People's Republic, and a growing awareness that imperialism was the enemy of all, even of the people of the countries that perpetuated it.

The Chinese speakers who preceded him had all received precisely punctuated shouts of approval, but either because of a language difficulty or because those forgathered in the square considered the Englishman's speech more a confession of guilt than a statement of principles, his words provoked only a heavy, uncomfortable silence. This caused him to become more abject and desperate, until he was finally reduced to a stammering apology for his own presence in Hong Kong.

As he went on, I began to be looked at by members of the crowd. Their eyes appraised me, turned back to the speaker, and then again to me, as if a connection were being perceived and pointed out between myself and the Englishman's act of contrition. I met these stares at first with the genial good manners of a foreigner in an alien place, but as the speaker's self-lacerations grew more maudlin and the stares more hostile, I struck an attitude that coldly disassociated myself from the untidy, remorseful figure on the platform. I walked through and on the edges of the crowd with a slow, imperial gait, looking straight ahead and smiling, creating a nonchalant and unregenerate presence. When I reached the corner of the square, I noticed a rickshaw stand tucked against the wall of a side street. I chose the carriage with the oldest driver, and, after giving him the name of my hotel, indicated that I wished to be drawn along a route adjacent to the rally. The man smiled, shrugged, and hoisted the pulling poles. He set off at a nicely paced trot, and, my arms spread out along the grimy wicker of the rickshaw seat, I made a complete tour of the square while the Englishman apologized for the past and the Chinese stared me out of their future. I, however, felt very much in the present, and I knew I was ready to begin gambling again.

Although gambling is not legal in Hong Kong, I had discovered that a great deal of *sub rosa* action could be found if one knew where to look. Since I didn't, I decided to hire a guide, and I asked one of the clerks at the hotel desk to arrange this for me, specifying with oblique innuendos the sort of tour I wanted to make of the city.

That evening, when my guide met me in the hotel lobby, I was afraid my wishes had been misunderstood. Standing in front of me, announcing a welcome to Hong Kong in English that was only slightly colored by a warbling Chinese accent, was a young man of cherubic appearance, a boy, really, whose face was unmarked by any trace of the sort of knowledge I was seeking.

"You are, Sir, the man who wishes gambling?" he asked. The suit he wore, though decorated with stains and mendings, was buttoned and worn with pride, as was the clean shirt glowing with starch that he left open at the neck.

When I acknowledged I was the one he sought, he sighed and then smiled, I thought, a little sadly, as he firmly held out his hand and introduced himself. His name, he said, was Peter Lee, and then, as if this, too, were part of his official introduction, he added that he was a member of the Congregationalist Church. Having thus presented himself, he led me to my car, held the door for me, and took his position gravely behind the wheel.

"Do you wish right away to begin gambling?" he asked. The last word of his question was slurred, as though he were afraid it might be overheard.

"Well, I haven't eaten. Perhaps, Peter, you know a good restaurant where there's also a roulette wheel?"

"Excuse me?"

"A place where one can have dinner and gamble too?"

"Oh, no," Peter quickly answered, staring at me curiously in the rear-view mirror. "The places where gambling is played have very unacceptable food. I could not recommend them to you, Sir."

"Well, there's no rush. Let's have a good dinner first."

"A fine idea, Sir," Peter said brightly, and in the mirror I saw something like relief flow across his eyes.

As we rode, Peter began to list the virtues of the restaurant he was guiding me to. While we crossed the harbor on a ferry, fought side street traffic, and wended our way up and down the suburban sides of mountains, he taxed himself and his English vocabulary with descriptions of sauces, noodles, and rare concoctions of fowl, fish and pig. Words like "piquant," "tart," and "pungent" were brought forth after long pauses of concentration and with evident pleasure over their evocative correctness. At first, I enjoyed his display of culinary English, but as it went on into the areas of arcane side dishes and exotic desserts, I began to grow impatient. It had been nearly an hour since we set off from the hotel, and we were now wandering in a neighborhood of dark streets and shuttered windows where it seemed unlikely that a restaurant such as Peter had been describing would be found.

"Your English is very impressive," I said, cutting in on his attempt to pinpoint the savor of a jellied spice cake.

"I was taught by the English church members," Peter answered with a modest ducking of the head. "And most of the people the agency sends me to guide are American."

"And are you ever going to guide this American to a restaurant?"

My tone made Peter's neck and shoulders stiffen.

"But, Sir, we are here already," he answered politely.

Peter led the way through an unmarked, doorless entrance into the restaurant's single room, which was lit and appointed like a public lavatory. About half a dozen tables were set against the walls, their tops bare of any signs of utensils or hospitality. They were all empty except for one at which sat several men in undershirts who picked rapidly with chopsticks at a common mound of food. On one of the walls there was a picture of an ancient, bearded mandarin; on the other, a portrait of Mao Tse-tung.

"The picture of Chairman Mao," Peter whispered, "is only for the benefit of those customers who may be sympathetic. It has nothing to do with the food."

One of the undershirted men came over to us and a long, intense conversation took place between him and Peter. The shifts in pitch and volume of their language made it seem an argument was being sung; however, when the man turned away, my guide announced that he had taken the liberty of ordering for me; the discussion had been simply about the menu. Then, although I protested, he insisted on waiting outside, as it was against company policy for guides to share their charges' table.

I sat down and waited. The room was silent except for the wet noises made by the men across the room. They ate voraciously, their eyes on the next morsel while they sucked and chewed the present one. I tried not to look at them, and the only time they noticed me was when I was caught in their scan of food. I began to feel uneasy. Why had Peter brought me to this place? How could someone so sensitive in his descriptions of tastes bring me, in my tailored and spotless suit of linen, to such a squalid room? My guide's face suddenly became less innocent, and I tried to reassure myself by recalling the denomination of the church he belonged to. Congregationalist. A Calvinist then, a Chinese Calvinist. This was not comforting; indeed, it increased the sense of menace I was beginning to feel.

I was thinking of leaving when the man who, through

Peter, took my order, returned with a trayful of condiments and a small dish containing my first course. He grinned in a way that indicated something rare was about to be displayed; then, slowly, he drew away the freckled porcelain cover and revealed a quartet of tiny roasted fowls perched on bushes of thinly chopped lettuce. Droplets of sweat from his forehead fell in and around the dish as he carefully indicated which of the little sauce bowls should serve as auxiliaries to the cooked birds.

The fumes that rose from the dish were seducing, and I picked up one of the birds in my fingers, dipped it into a dark red broth, and took a cautious bite from its breast. My palate and suspicions were both disarmed. Taste buds that for years had lain dormant, stupefied by alcohol and tobacco, woke in celebration of the flesh that passed over them, and the genial contentment that fine aliment spreads through the mind made me forget all thoughts of plots and collusion.

I had just finished stacking a pile of closely gnawed bones on a plate provided for that purpose, when the second course, dumplings, floating serenely in a lemon-scented sauce, was placed in front of me; and when this was dispatched, I found myself stared at by the eye of a medium-sized fish, its body covered by a latticework of scallions surrounded by a foamy sea of rice and peapods.

And so it went, course following immediately upon course. When I left the restaurant, I had gorged myself into an amiable torpor. Peter smiled as he watched me slide across the car's rear seat, and I complimented his choice of restaurant with a long moan of satisfaction.

I was taken next to a small nightclub where drinks were served at the bar two at a time and a Chinese chanteuse, accompanied by piano, drums and violin, sang medleys of American songs in Cantonese.

Still wobbly from dinner, I tried to unclot my mind and

body with large tumblers of brandy. As I began to feel less sated, I also became flushed and pleasantly unfocused.

"Where does one gamble here?" I finally asked Peter, assuming my eyes were missing the telltale signs of a secret room. He stood behind my stool, not drinking, but allowed by office rules to keep me company as long as I did not sit down at a table.

"Is it not somewhat amusing to hear Chinese words to your music?" he asked. A look of anticipation crossed his face, as though he expected a long conversation to issue from his question.

"Cards, Peter! Dice, roulette!"

A prim, hurt look came into his eyes.

"I thought you would wish a peaceful digestion after such a meal."

He took me then to a theater club where he said he had heard games of chance were also played. Since there were only tables, I sat alone for a while watching a troupe of acrobats perform tumbles and feats of delicate balance. A girl brought a bottle of champagne to my table, demanded payment, and smiled dumbly when I asked about the possibility of one's luck being tried in her establishment. When I left, the acrobats had danced on rubber balls, walked on their fingers, and formed a human pyramid, and I had transformed my after-dinner sluggishness into a relaxed and slightly drunk curiosity.

This time Peter actually apologized for the absence of gambling, as well as for the hundred-dollar price for the obligatory champagne.

"It doesn't matter," I told him, for I was still not sure whether he was a bumbling guide or a calculating shill. "It was served by a very pretty girl."

"Ah, very pretty. I understand."

His understanding brought us to another nightclub, this

time with a cavernous ballroom and an invisible orchestra. Lanterns floated in the darkness; women brushed by one like moths, unseen, with a fluttery touch of one's face and fingers. And when the touch was returned, one was led out beneath the lanterns and into movement to the music. If all went well, one then danced, literally danced, with one's partner into small, curtained-off rooms where, instead of the artifacts of gambling, one found obscene murals, mirrored ceilings, and large, loosely made beds.

After this stop, I was in neither the mood nor the condition to make any more demands about gambling. Either through ignorance or design, Peter had spent the whole night beguiling my senses and avoiding the destination he'd been hired to lead me to. Whatever the reason for his subterfuge, it was obviously strong enough to keep him determined to mislead me for the rest of the night. I had him take me back to the hotel, and surprised him by making arrangements to meet the following evening.

Peter met me at the same time, at the same place, and in the same suit. I repeated my instructions of the night before, and, as though there were no memory of his having failed to carry them out, he nodded and led me once more to our car.

Hong Kong is made up of several islands and a patch of mainland Asia, so that traveling about the city involves many ferry rides. While we were on one of these short boat trips, both Peter and I left the car and stood by the deck's railing, breathing in the cool air and sour odor of the harbor. Around us people sat and stared at the sky or took slow, stretching walks along the deck. A fine spray settled on and cooled one's face. Quietly suspended between the shores of the city, the ferry was a perfect place for a gentle interrogation.

Peter stood next to me, staring intently at the boat's spumy wake and the dark water into which it disappeared. He seemed to sense he was about to be challenged, and had set himself in a defiant posture, his shoulders back and hands clenched at his sides.

"Peter, are you really taking me to a place to gamble?"

"I am a guide," he answered coldly. "I will take you wherever you want."

"You didn't last night."

"You did not enjoy yourself?"

"That isn't the point, Peter."

For the first time that night, my guide looked directly at me.

"I hate gambling," he said, slowly and bitterly. "I do not want to guide anyone to it."

I hadn't expected this blunt reason, and the hatred in Peter's eyes convinced me that he had expressed something more personal than a moral objection.

"If you feel this way, why did you accept the job?"

Suddenly, his resolute attitude began to weaken, and he looked fearful.

"You are angry, Sir? You will fire me?"

I told him that I had no intention of sending him away with a bad report, that I was only curious. He stared at me as though judging whether I was telling the truth; then, after a deep breath, he began, in a rush of confused narrative, to explain why he had misled me the night before.

At first, it seemed his objections were moral after all. He said that, as a Christian, he believed it was his duty to protect those whom he guided, not merely from padded bills and tourist traps, but also from the deeper evils of Hong Kong, the worst of which was the gambling den. Gluttony, intemperance, fornication, into all of which he admitted having led me the previous night, were trivial threats to the soul compared to the perils involved in wagering on games of chance. Therefore, when word came to his agency that a stranger in the city intended to put himself willfully in such jeopardy, he, Peter, had felt called upon to prevent him, even if that meant distracting him with lesser sins.

As I listened, I had to be amused that I might have been thwarted, on this island in the China seas, by old prejudices of the Geneva consistory, which, if I remembered correctly, ranked card-playing a greater offense than adultery. The amusement faded, however, when Peter began a transition from the Christian to the personal. Standing stiffly, his hands grasping the brass railing, he told me how, as a child, he had come to know the infernal world of gamblers.

"My father lost me," he said. "First it was my mother, then my very beautiful sister, then he lost me."

It took me some minutes and several questions fully to understand what Peter meant by being "lost." In ruptured, stammered sentences, he told me how his father, a teacher of high school sciences, had begun gambling, and how he had one day covered the walls of the apartment they lived in with charts of lunar phases, horoscopic signs, and other perversions of the disciplines he earned his living from. Shortly after, voices began to speak to him, and he to them. Hunches were whispered, and secret rituals worked out which, if rigorously performed, would bring success at fan-tan, poker, and the race track.

Peter had been only eleven then, and he had understood nothing except the horror of seeing his father deceived by his voices and gradually stripped of everything he was and owned. Slumped over the side of the boat, his body trembling, Peter then told me how, one night, while the family sat on the floor of a room now empty of everything except a cooking pot and a few blankets, three men had come to the apartment, professional gamblers and members of a syndicate to which his father had lost so much that the only way he had of paying his debt was by putting his wife at their disposal. There had been no arguments when the three men appeared. His mother had simply left, carrying nothing of her own, with these men who now owned her until someone discharged the debt for which she had been placed in pawn. A month or so later, the same men came for Peter's sister, and shortly after that for Peter himself. This time his father had wept, but Peter had only found the attitude of grief horrible to look at, and had wished his father dead.

For the next two years he worked in menial ways for this organization of professional gamblers. He was treated neither with kindness nor contempt, but only as an object of specific value that was part of the syndicate's general reckoning of profits.

But even syndicates are subject to bad runs of luck, and during one of these, Peter was lost to a woman gambler who accepted him as payment for a night's success at roulette. Then, when her luck turned, she passed him on to one of her creditors, along with a pair of pearl bracelets. His new owner, an old man with an addiction to blackjack, soon lost Peter once more to the same syndicate that had won him from his father.

Peter might have shuttled back and forth between winners and losers in the world of Hong Kong gambling forever, had not difficulties with the authorities caused the syndicates to become less imaginative in the ways in which they paid and collected their debts. The police would tolerate gambling, as long as human beings were no longer to be used as stakes. Peter, therefore, suddenly became a useless item of exchange, and one of the syndicate chiefs humanely deposited him in an orphanage run by a mission of the Evangelical Church. There Peter was tutored in the mysteries of predestination, the elect, and the reasons behind God's allowing the demons of gambling to exist.

The ferry had landed and we were again in our car when

Peter finished his tale by saying he had never seen his mother, sister or father again. He was then silent, waiting, I suppose, for my sympathetic response. However, I only felt curiously repelled by the story he had told me, and I resented the absurdity of such a squalid parable having been offered me for my own good.

The car stopped in front of a small building with a glowing sign over its door spelling the name "The Happy Moon." A large, full selenic face of red and white light floated over the letters, grinning maliciously. Peter glanced up at it, and then looked away.

"There is really gambling here, Sir."

For a moment, a very short moment, I felt I should return to the hotel, find another guide, and begin again. However, when I noticed how intently Peter watched me, I smiled confidently back at the neon moon and got out of the car.

"Must you go?" Peter asked. There was no doubt from the look he gave me that he was sincerely frightened.

"I *want* to go, Peter," I said to him.

"But you will lose!"

"That's a rude thing to say," I replied coldly. It was also an unlucky thing to say, but I put that out of mind as I left Peter and walked quickly into The Happy Moon.

At first, it seemed my guide had again misled me: except for two Americans sitting morosely at the bar, and a few girls waiting patiently in booths for customers, The Happy Moon appeared quiet and empty. The only noise in the room came from the hundreds of little moons hanging from the ceiling on invisible wires—half-moons, crescent moons, gibbous moons—which produced muted clicks and ringings as, swayed by hidden fans, they collided gently with one another.

Then suddenly a rumble of groans and laughter came from behind a curtain at the rear of the bar. It lasted barely a second and then disappeared, but I had heard enough to recognize the choral sounds of gamblers, the special harmony produced by winners and losers at the turn of a card. When I pushed past the curtain, I found myself stepping into what looked, at first, like a bank vault. Bars running from floor to ceiling blocked off the open side of a brightly lit room, the walls of which were marked with golden draperies and high silk screens. A glass chandelier, too large for the ceiling's height, gleamed oppressively over the heads of the half-dozen men and one woman who sat, money stacked in front of them, in the highback chairs around a long banquet table. In front of the bars, a trimly built Indian, in a costume colonial uniform and military turban, stood guard. He stepped aside in order that those on the other side of the bars might see the new arrival. The men, except for one young Chinese in a velvet dinner jacket, were all Americans or Europeans. They looked at me indifferently while the woman at the head of the table smiled and shuffled a deck of cards. She was Eurasian, with a handsome face made up of jovial lines and soft, mischievous features. Wig, powder and rouge enshrouded her age, but her voice was that of an old woman.

"Fresh blood. Let him in."

With this common greeting of a new player the bars were opened by the Indian, and I took a seat at the end of the table. The gates closed with a snap behind me.

"Minimum bet, one hundred dollars Hong Kong," the woman said, the long, loose sleeves of the high-collared robe she wore flapping over her hands as she continued to shuffle. "Maximum, one thousand."

The rate of exchange was then approximately five Hong Kong for one American dollar, and I put four hundred of the latter on the table in front of me and asked the name of the game we were playing. The woman laughed at my having so boldly sat down without knowing such an important fact, and the men politely spread the amusement around the table while I was informed that the game was blackjack and told the local rules of play. I made a minimum bet, and cards were dealt to everyone except the Chinese; the woman had to glide the cards a long way across the table's surface and it was the Oriental's job to follow quickly behind them, retrieving any stray throws, checking the accuracy of the players' wagers, and collecting and paying when the hand was over. He moved so silently and deftly, that one would not have noticed him at all if he hadn't scented himself with a cloying perfume whose heavy odor entranced the brain each time he tiptoed behind one's chair.

Well, I thought, you have found your game. You are in a backroom in Asia; you have just been, by a fundamentalist Chinese Christian, warned of the evil of your enterprise; the empress dealing has silk sleeves ample enough to hide several decks of cards and much chicanery; her minion sweetly poisons the air around you; and you are caged in with strangers and guarded by a Gurkha. You are gambling, indeed.

When, three hours later, I left The Happy Moon, Peter greeted me with a cold and wary expression. He did not open the car door for me, and as I did so, his eyes searched me intently for the effects of my having directly exposed myself to the infections of gambling. I sat calmly in the back seat until he finished his scrutiny and took his place behind the wheel. It was not until we had driven for several blocks that I withdrew a thick packet of notes from my inside coat pocket—more than twenty thousand dollars Hong Kong— and told him I had won.

Won, however, is a meager summary. From the very first hand, the game had gently enfolded me, delivering up winning cards in a way that undid the rights of luck and rules of probability. My fellow players watched with bitter wonder as I drained away the table's good fortune. Two of them, Englishmen, declared that they felt themselves the victims of a tasteless joke, and left the room; while the Chinese began to mutter testily as he drifted back and forth with my winnings, and the rank smell of petulance became mixed with the stench of his perfume. His mistress endured my luck for a long while before her composure broke, but finally, she too, soured, and began cursing each time I turned over blackjacks, drew fives to counts of sixteen, and trios of tens to thrice-split aces.

Strangely, I'd felt no flashes of glory as I had when winning in Las Vegas, nor had I found a need for allegory, heroes, *belles dames* or villains. There'd been no sharp drama in what had happened, but rather a serene sense of inevitability. Finally, it had begun to seem so natural a thing to win, that I became embarrassed by the simplicity of it all. I had quit the game when I felt it would have been obscene for me to draw another winning hand.

"I am glad you won, Sir," Peter said when we were in front of the hotel. He had not spoken at all during the drive home, and his voice was flat and unenthusiastic.

"I am too," I said slowly and emphatically. Then, to make my success palpable to Peter, I again removed the bundle of money from my pocket. Peter stared at my treasure curiously, but remained unimpressed. After all, each time he had been lost, there had been someone to win him. He had seen victories before.

"Shall I come tomorrow?" he asked.

"I don't think I can go back to the same place," I told him.

"I know others," he said crisply, and then turned and walked back to the car.

I found it hard to fall asleep that night. The memory of the game's perfection disturbed me, and I began to wonder if I hadn't been given a kindly sign to stop pressing my claims upon fate and to accept the evening's flawless performance as my farewell to gambling. After all, lesser victories in the past had been followed by heavy failures. There was a deadly balance to chance, an exacting alternation that I had no real reason to believe I had overcome. It was not until I promised myself to be wary, cautious and suspicious of the slightest signs of reversal that I felt justified in relaxing into sleep.

But conquest continued to be easy. The next night, in a room devoted to roulette, I experienced the same effortless good fortune. The players at the table were all Chinese, and since I won without great expense of energy, I had leisure to study the excitability and verve of the Oriental gambler. Only one table was in play, but the eight or nine men standing around it babbled at such a volume and bet with such frantic gesticulations that it seemed a full casino was in use. One gambler would smash a pile of chips down on a number and then, during the wheel's spin, move his wager to a dozen different numbers; another would argue and scuffle with his partner over which color would wear their bet until a Chinese *rien ne va plus* forced a decision; others threw fistfuls of chips at random on the table, accepting where they came to rest as fateful places; and one, a very ancient man dressed in a pajama-like suit and derby hat, would lean directly over the turning wheel and, his face inches from the blurred surface. scream orders at the small white ball as it bounced among the numbered grooves.

At first, they seemed to resent my presence, but when they saw how fine my instincts were for the right columns, colors and numbers, odd and even, they began to pile their chips alongside mine on the squares and rectangles I marked for them. When I left, most of them followed me out into the street, entreating me to stay. Peter, horrified at the society I dragged behind me, had to subdue his countrymen with fierce gestures and hard language before I could enter the car and lock the doors behind me.

The next night, I guessed, with the same supernal luck, the count of beans in a fan-tan parlor; and in the evenings that followed, I won at chemin de fer, roulette, and again at blackjack. When I told Peter that I felt ready for some more exotic forms of Oriental gambling, he took me to an abandoned building in a squalid neighborhood where lizards, beetles, frogs and worms of hideous aspect and great length competed against their kind across courses marked by strings and bottles on a sandy floor. By this time, Peter had begun shyly accompanying me to the games themselves, and he watched, repelled and fascinated, as I selected winning amphibians, insects and annelids, and caused awe and respect among the riffraff and degenerate gamblers of a Hong Kong slum.

As we were about to leave, I noticed a large circle being formed around a solemn-looking man dressed in long white robes who was calmly removing, one by one, snakes from a large straw basket he had strapped to his waist. Each serpent, about two feet in length, was held up and stretched to its full extension, so that it could be appraised by the ring of gamblers. While this took place, an assistant put a small marking of paint on the head of each of the snakes to distinguish them, for they were all temple vipers, with near-identical green-and-yellow colorings.

When all the snakes had been displayed, they were returned to the basket while an assistant went to fetch a small rodent which he placed in a cage at the circle's center. Then, once more, the snakes were removed, this time to be selected and wagered on by the gamblers.

I watched and listened to the betting, wondering whether I could win at even this grotesque use of chance. Then, as it was being fondled by its owner, one of the snakes coiled quickly about his arm and thrust its body in a long, undulating suspension toward me. The flat, hard, emerald head came to a quivering rest a few feet from my face, and from its eyes I felt a cold, lucid, direct communication.

I forced Peter, who stood shuddering next to me, to bet all my night's winnings on this viper, and then enjoyed his horror and amazement as my snake, when placed on the ground among its brothers, slithered with ominous purpose toward the caged rodent, struck lethally between the bars, and won, with great appetite, the wager I had put on him.

After that evening, besides joining me at the tables, Peter's attitude began changing in other ways. The stiff, melancholy disapproval of my gambling began to give way to a vicarious involvement in it. At first he was fearful, trembling at every large bet I made, seeing in it a potential dark moment, an imminent reversal of fortune that would bring upon me the same fate as those gamblers who had owned and lost him in the past. But gradually, as I continued to win, his anxiousness disappeared, replaced by an excited curiosity about my methods and manners while gambling. I would notice him studying me, smiling and nodding to himself, as if he had found a fine shade of meaning in the way I fondled chips or arranged a hand of cards. Occasionally, when I caught his eye while the outcome of a bet was being decided, he would seem to nod and flash a wink of understanding, as if he had just then discovered a clue to the hidden reason for my success. When we talked, it was now always about gambling, and I felt a polite but firm probing on Peter's part to confirm some sort of belief in a secret I possessed, a power which I had somehow acquired and through which I could penetrate the patterns of a deal of blackjack or a serpent's mind.

But I believed in no secrets. I felt, without vanity, that

this was the way I was meant to exist. The separateness I had felt in my ride through the Communist crowd in a rickshaw was dissolving; but I was not joining the multitude, it was joining me. I felt I had truly acquired a presence that drew the world to it, and the disjunctions of thought and surroundings, of my past and my location, began to fade. The city I was in, the water and mountains around it, the faces and manners of its crowds, were becoming parts of my own continuous experience.

The culmination of this feeling came one morning as I stood on the crest of Hong Kong's highest mountain, Victoria Peak, staring at the scattered ships beneath me in the harbor and the bleary expanse of ocean and continent spread out around them. I had gambled and sensualized until dawn; I felt raw from fatigue, and full of an almost painful energy that the night's excesses had been unable to dissipate.

Gradually, as more and more light crept across the harbor, everything began to seem designed for my gaze, the contours and colors of the view unfolding for my special pleasure. The shape of city and countryside became precise and palpable; the sky and water hued with colors that begged my eyes' attention. And then, in the middle of this harmonizing to the pitch of my senses, as the coast and mountains extended themselves gently to embrace me, other images from a different scenery blended with those of the island I was on, images remembered from another time in my life when I had known a sensory alliance with the world.

As a soldier in Germany, I had spent a few days on a walking tour of the countryside around the small town I'd been temporarily assigned to. This had been an odd impulse for me, since, at the time, everything I desired was in the cities of the world. When I began, I felt uncomfortably out of place, as in hiking boots, *Spazierhosen* and rucksack, I trekked

235

through rustic settings and affected tremors of appreciation at the sight of a shadowed grove or an early-morning forest mist. However, by the second day of strolling, my urban eye stopped seeing only the flat, postcard beauty of nature, and began to perceive its essential luster. This change took place while I was walking between the towns of Bad Orb and Gelnhausen, through the Barbarossa Valley, along a narrow depression of harrowed, filemot earth banked by soft, terraced hills, and though I knew how much history had preceded me across this bit of land, there were no battle echoes to distract me, no heroic ghosts to insist that everything be measured by human time. For the length of a day's walk, the Barbarossa Tal and I had formed a pure present and a tranquil unity.

Now in another corner of the earth that sense of an immediate perfection of the world returned after an absence of almost two decades, and as the German valley blended with the yellowing sky of an Oriental morning, I felt I held the whole earth in a clear and extensive view, and that not only the present prospect, but all those I had moved through in the past, were the correct and necessary settings for my life.

While I was enjoying this feeling of being well domiciled in the world, Peter had been sleeping in the car behind me. As I turned away from the view and began walking toward the car, something startled him awake. He looked bewildered and anxious until he saw me, and asked for the second time how much I had won during the night. When I told him, he smiled, nodded, and closed his eyes. Reassured that he was guide to one of the elect, he was now ready to return to and confront the nightmare from which he'd just fled.

Chapter X

"You dirty old man, all right!"

The speaker was Mei Su, a small young girl with a beautifully fragile face that sat like a little moon above a high, lace-purfled collar. The words in the judgment she pronounced upon me sounded like tiny bells being rung, and even if Peter had not explained that "dirty old man" was Mei Su's way of paying a compliment in English, I would have been charmed by the melody of her abuse. Still, it was reassuring to know that she referred to my crafty way of playing cards rather than my age and sexual habits.

Sitting next to Mei Su was Li Ming, also a girl of about eighteen. She had a grave, handsome face bordered by long dark hair that fell to her shoulders, and each time I turned a winning card, she would smile sadly to herself. Occasionally, with fingers so long and supple they seemed boneless, she would pick up the entire deck and silently examine the cards, gazing at them with a look that suggested she attrib-

237

uted to them the ability to change of themselves their pictures and markings.

We had been playing blackjack for dollars, and I was the house, letting the girls bet against me and winning, not from skill or trickery, but because they attacked the game with charming hunches and whims. Peter, who had brought me to meet these two friends of his, beamed with delight as I displayed to Mei Su and Li Ming the ways of a winning gambler.

While we played, Peter explained to me the history of my two opponents. They were cousins, both born in Shanghai and both from families that had difficult times under Mao's regime. Li Ming's father, a teacher like his own, had been accused of Confucianist tendencies during the Cultural Revolution and, after having been paraded in a dunce cap through the streets, had been sent to a remote rural province where he died while being reeducated. Li Ming then went with her mother to live with Mei Su's family. However, Mei Su's father was also in bad favor with the authorities due to old epicurean habits, which despite his loyalty to Marxist principles, he could not overcome. One of the Guardians of District Morals—such is the title Peter told me the government confers on those who bring it local counterrevolutionary gossip—reported seeing frozen ducks, cartons of whiskey, and other elitist items being delivered to Mei Su's house in a truck without official markings. An investigation showed that her father had been patronizing the black market, and it became expedient for him to bribe a few officials and escape with his family to Hong Kong.

Here they struggled like other uprooted Chinese families until the father tired of the effort and began, with the help of old contacts in Shanghai, smuggling contraband antiques from the Communist mainland into capitalist Hong Kong shops. This time he was the victim of a mercenary informer, and was sentenced to a short jail term, a humiliation that mortified the family. The older women wept, starved themselves into a stupor, and ended in a hospital where they withdrew from the world. Li Ming and Mei Su, faced with how to survive, made a pact to become rich and independent women through the one profession in Hong Kong that was now open to them.

For three years they worked as successful short-term concubines and bar girls, putting away in the process a sum of money with which they hoped to free themselves from service to others and begin some enterprise of their own. However, a year ago, while spending a professional weekend in Macao with—as Peter luridly put it—two black Madras Indians who wanted to try their luck at the casinos, Li and Mei Su succumbed to the spell of gambling, seeing in the flow of colored plaques and jetons a way to riches much faster and less capricious than that which they had been following. In order to play, they had borrowed from their escorts, and when they lost, they borrowed again, until by the end of their stay they were in debt for twice the amount they had saved, and no amount of skillful lovemaking could persuade the swarthy Indians to consider the money as simply another pleasurable expense. When they returned to Hong Kong, a reckoning was demanded, threats were made that ranged from mutilation to murder, and the terrified girls, with neither pimps nor police to protect them, had paid, and were still paying, the gentlemen from Madras. In effect, they would be working for these—again Peter's words —curry-smelling Hindus for the next three or four years unless something miraculous happened.

While Peter told the story, and Mei Su embellished it, her cousin spoke not at all, but at appropriate moments would widen her eyes and twist her face into grimaces so that she looked like a Chinese mask meant to frighten devils away from the ceremonies of men.

"She always scared now and make ugly faces," Mei Su said, putting her arm around her cousin. "She no like selling ass every night to different fellow to pay off sonsabitch Indians. Hey, you know before we go to Macao and lose, we just had good, dirty old men who keep us three, four months at a time. That not so bad, but three, four times a night—that make my cousin sick, and she cries when she sleep and speaks such a little when she awake."

Li Ming began to shudder, and when she tried to gather up the scattered cards, her hands shook too violently for her to hold them. Embarrassed, she locked her pliant fingers together and tried to stare them into stillness. Mei Su and Peter spoke softly to her in Chinese while she fought to keep her face from forming yet another aspect of terror.

"You see, Sir," Peter said to me, "we have all three suffered from gambling. That is why we are friends. But you, Sir, you live from gambling, you are made happy by it. You understand its secrets."

What I was beginning to understand, was the reason for the meeting.

"You win all our dollars faster even than Macao casino," Mei Su added.

"You lost," I said to Mei Su, "because you don't understand how to play, not because of any secrets I have."

"Oh, we know there are numbers to be learned about gambling," Peter said. "But isn't there more to it than numbers? It must be, for my father knew them and it did him no good."

As I accepted this in silence, Li Ming raised her eyes from her folded hands and looked directly at me.

"It is not what you know, it is you," she said softly.

Mei Su and Peter looked at Li Ming, waiting to see if she would say anything more. When she again lowered her gaze, Peter sighed and told me what they wanted from me.

"We would like you to gamble for us," he said. "We will give you the money, and you will lend us your luck—only, of course, for a short time."

"Just until we take back two times what goddamnshit Macao casino take from us," Mei Su sang to me.

So they wanted me to be their auspice, to turn my winning streak into an act of philanthropy. They had no idea of the danger this would put me in. Luck cannot be shared, and to try to do so means risking its vanishing altogether. I was about to tell them no, but then I noticed in the three pairs of eyes something I'd wanted to inspire since I began gambling: the moist, languid look of worship. Against all better judgment, lured on by holy admiration, I let myself become their demiurge of gambling, their deliverer from the failures of fathers and a protector against the plots of two dark Indians from the Coromandel Coast.

Later, in the cousin's small apartment, after allegiances had been pledged with glasses of vodka, Peter took me aside and, in a solemn, slurred voice, told me that, because of my conquests of the gambling halls of Hong Kong, he no longer believed in evil demons. He toasted and thanked me for having helped him to become a better Christian, and then, putting his glass down carefully, he asked me if I prayed before and during gambling, and though I told him the nature of my prayers was not orthodox, he seemed satisfied that it was an expedient thing to do and announced that he was going home to send his thoughts heavenwards before he became unconscious from the vodka. When I started to leave with him, he looked shocked, and directed my attention to Li Ming and Mei Su, who were perched on the edge of a quilt-covered mattress that had been quietly set on the floor while Peter and I were talking. By each of its corners, candles had been placed in roseate jars, and shadows and flames danced an invitation across the girls' faces. I looked at Peter, but he was backing toward the door, a finger raised to smiling lips and a look on his face that suggested tolerance of the sins about to be committed.

Forsaking her rude English, Mei Su whispered in Chinese as she guided me to the little bed and drew me down upon it. The removal of shoes, jacket, shirt and pants was accompanied by these unintelligible bursts of verbal melody, and the room slowly darkened as Li Ming, the frenzy in her eyes now softened, cupped one by one the candle flames in her hand and blew them softly out. Then, hidden in darkness, the palps of twenty fingers and four palms began to probe and caress the body of a dirty old man, the wise and wily sorcerer of gambling.

It was hours later when I was awakened by Li Ming's scream. She was coiled like a torqued wire next to me, fear rippling across her body while she slept. As I stroked her and felt the flutter of delicate muscles beneath her damp skin, I thought how, unlike Peter, I wanted to believe in demons and in the clear and simple evil they represented. Let good be myriad, elusive and unattainable, if only evil could be shaped for an honest encounter.

In the dark I tried to body forth such an adversary, but could conjure up nothing but old, comic gargoyles and sentimental portraits of myself.

The speedboat we had hired for the trip to Macao leaped and splashed across the water, and even Li Ming joined in the laughter as the sea spray, cool and stinging, blew over us. We were in the open water, the South China Sea, and in the distance Hong Kong became a white, receding haze. Standing at the wheel, an old man of indeterminate nationality, dressed in pajamas and a soiled yachting cap, led us through fishing fleets, past lumbering freighters, and into races with Hovercrafts and yachts bound for the same port as we. Close around us were dark verdant islands that rose as single mountains from the sea; and farther to the west, illumined by an orange sun, was the long, deep coast of mainland China, tacked onto which, some fifty miles south, was a pustule of colonialism, the Portuguese port of Macao. Once famous as a refuge for visa-revoked sinners from the Malay Peninsula to the Sea of Japan, it was now an island of gambling casinos known for their high limits and lavish settings.

I had expected such a port to be shrouded in a miasmal fog, but instead, when it appeared, a soft green shoreline rose clearly in the sunlight, and as we grew nearer, clusters of pink villas came into view. Despite these benign, pastel colors, the memories and reputation of Macao made my three companions watchful and silent as our boat cruised alongside the dock and the old pilot struck a figurehead's attitude and announced we had arrived.

In two pedicabs we proceeded along a quiet, empty seaside road that ran past rows of shuttered, walled-in houses, the courtyards of which, with gardens and statued fountains, could be glimpsed through filigreed iron gates. One saw the churches, too, the familiar architectures of Christian faith. However, they looked shut and unattended, and one of them, of a soft baroque style, was nothing but a facade, its open portal leading neither to nave nor altar, but into a barren field.

Although it was now past noon, the town was not fully awake. A few Chinese sat in chairs in front of their shops, sunning themselves and chatting across narrow cobbled streets. Small, shady paseos were without strollers, their benches empty except for a few old men and women sharing bowls of food. Only when we turned into a square where

Communist schoolchildren were performing calisthenics, a choreography of exercise that included banner-waving and cadenced shouting, was there any vitality to the Macao morning. As we passed, Mei Su waved and shouted something in Chinese to the students, but they were too disciplined to notice. Only their instructor turned to give us a contemptuous look.

I was still watching the students when Mei Su squealed again and Peter stiffened and clutched the briefcase in which he carried his and the girls' money. The cabs had turned and come to a wharf; and there, moored in front of us, was the casino.

It was a chilling monstrosity: a giant chinoiserie riverboat with dragons rising from its hull, and lights and lanterns running from its stacks down to the railings of its three decks. A long, canopied gangplank funneled gamblers on and off the boat, and around its entrance, people milled, begged and bartered. Some sold betting systems; some charms and charts of fortune; but most simply demanded money and howled reminders of the rewards of charity. Away from the edges of the crowd were little clumps of children, waiting, as I later saw, to spring in pursuit of chips thrown from the boat by generous winners.

For a while, my three companions and I were caught in the throng, unable to push our way to the boat's entrance. Peter, his arms wrapped around the bag of money, stared sadly at the faces of the men who begged and touted. Li Ming and Mei Su pulled at me impatiently, as though I had only to give a sign and a path would be made for us. I was not, however, anxious to go on board. I was repelled by the vessel in front of us, by its dreadnought size and *Narrenschiff* aspect; a mockery of ships that made real voyages in the world.

Finally, police appeared at the gangplank and the crowd

temporarily scattered. Led by the cousins, with Peter pushing behind me, we went onto the ship and into the gambling room of the main deck. It was enormous, with ceilings high enough to contain giant potted bamboo trees, and though it was now early afternoon, men and women were packed around a hundred tables, playing all the games of chance of the civilized world.

"How wonderful," Peter said. "I cannot even see where it ends."

This was so. The dimensions of the casino were such that the lines of card and roulette tables stretched out of sight.

"Was that the bad luck table?" Mei Su asked, pointing to a roulette table like all the others. Her cousin didn't remember. "Yes, that's the place," Mei Su said, scowling at the offending wheel and furniture. Then to me: "You play there. You win our money back from where we piss it."

She wanted vengeance even on the inanimate objects that took her savings, and since I would not plead superstition as an excuse, we approached the guilty table, and Peter opened his case and handed me twenty thousand Hong Kong dollars. Then he closed his eyes and mumbled something vaguely imprecatory. Mei Su and Li Ming, as an earnest of their faith and affection, each took one of my hands and placed it firmly over her right breast. Thus fortified and honored, I moved to the edge of the table, and when I exchanged the money given me for chips, the amount impressed one of the floor attendants so that he firmly lifted an old martingale player from one of the chairs and beckoned me to take his place. I sat down just as a spin was beginning. Wheel and ball moved for a time in separate directions, the ball holding to the wheel's inclining side through the force of its propulsion and the friction of its path. Then after a slow, rolling slide, it dropped and bounced among the wheel's compartments. The noise at the table rose, and, like the derby-hatted man in Hong Kong, several Chinese leaned toward the spinning wheel and shouted at it last-minute warnings and reminders.

The fingers that grasped my brain squeezed sharply, and in a painless blink of time, the sure connection I had come to know between myself and my setting vanished. In its place was now a sudden strangeness, an odd imbalance to everything around me. There was a subtle danger now in each person I looked at, as if I and those at the table with me no longer shared the same laws of matter. Costumes, movements, faces, sounds—all were now discordant and distorted human data, out-of-joint images that my mind could not mend. I could not tell whether a spell had been lifted or put upon me. I knew where I was, but no longer the reason for my being there.

A second convulsion followed the first; this time of fear, a biting intimation that something dreadful awaited. I was wrenched out of my own dramatic sheath, and saw myself, roleless and vulnerable, sitting among barbaric creatures that were now immune to my powers of invention. I understood that, if I lost, I would be utterly alone, deserted even by my own imagination. And I was certain I would lose, not only the money my followers had entrusted to me, but my own as well. Base, crude pictures appeared of the stacks of cash and checks I had placed in banks and deposit boxes, and I viewed them now as gloriously tangible things. The thought of their being taken from me, of even a tenth of my treasures being lost through casual guesses on cards or numbers, now horrified me. In the middle of success and singular adventure, I had suddenly lost both the imagination and the heart to gamble.

Of course, I fought against this abjection. I tried to summon forth bursts of high-minded contempt for my money and my life, tried to glamourize fear with images of romantic ruin and swaggering defeat. But my fear could neither be refuted nor fashionably dressed. It was down-to-earth and brutal; it wanted me to know my place and flee the table and room I was in. Yet I did not move, did not let myself succumb completely to this contemptible seizure. I thought I could will myself to bet, force the chips in front of me through the barrier of terror and practical sense until they were in play. When I placed my hands around them, however, the little discs would not be budged; I hadn't even the strength to topple them at random across the table. Even if I could have moved them, my mind would not have been able to select their destination, for it saw in every inch of the table's betting surface a sly, pervasive danger. Numerals, squares, letters—all took on the contours of treachery. There was nowhere a risk could be taken without the anticipation of defeat.

And so I sat, slumped and immobile, trying to make my paralysis assume an attitude of calculation and control. I tried to believe that what was happening was natural, that the hidden effects of so many bets and their attendant passions had simply worn down my will to play. That this break in my spirit should happen so suddenly, without warning, and after the long calm of a winning streak, should not be surprising. Unnoticed wounds were now demanding their toll, that was all. It wasn't me sitting transfixed at the table, it was only a morbid effigy created by long-abused nerves.

But the fear would not let me rest with this soft diagnosis. It demanded I see more in its presence than a momentary lack of character. It charged me to experience, with malicious precision, a sense of myself as a dim and ordinary item of the world, as much a lucent hero of chance as the ball that bounced from groove to groove on the wheel spinning in front of me. And the ball was at least immune to the needs of human survival. But I, what was I doing roaming the world at random, playing at life when it was such a serious business? No, I had to learn to be still, accumulate, be crafty, and survive.

Thus I sat, immobile, while the wheel turned and I made no bet. Mei Su, hunched next to my knee, her hand gently caressing my groin, understood something was wrong and sweetly tried to revive in me a sense of purpose. Peter, standing behind my chair, asked again and again in warm, breathy whispers why I didn't bet. But they, too, now seemed part of the general menace around me. I didn't know them any longer, nor could I find any reason for them to be so closely pressed against me.

"If you're not going to play, then let me," Peter said, his voice sharp with impatience. This offer somehow released me, and I rose from the chair at the same time he slipped into it. I watched just long enough to see him place on red the stack of chips that I'd been unable to move. His manner was confident, almost brutal, and he stared with a comical disdain at the wheel when it began to spin. I left the table and walked through the crowd, finally reaching one of the deck restaurants. I sat down at an empty table, and in a few moments Li Ming joined me. Her face, as she stared at me, seemed calmer than I'd ever seen it, almost serene with wisdom. But I would not let myself trust the flow of sympathy I felt coming from her. No, we had nothing in common at that moment, except, perhaps, that we were both now lightly acquainted with madness.

Li Ming and Mei Su each held one of my arms as we walked back toward the wharf of the main harbor where our boat was moored. Peter, a few feet in front of us, stepping backwards so he could deliver a full-face address, clutched his satchel in his arms and recounted joyously the details of his first gambling adventures. He had won, well over twice the amount that had been our goal, and he wanted us to know exactly why he had been certain that red would appear for a fourth consecutive time, or how, after betting only even chances, he had known to plunge heavily on the number 23. I listened to his beginner's boasting, and understood that Peter believed that he had finally won himself back; he was no longer someone else's stake or wager. I had only a few hours ago believed the same about myself, and I was still noble enough not to begrudge this belief in others.

Now, with each step we took away from the casino, the fear diminished, and the chaos of impressions that had assaulted me began to settle back into sensible patterns. I was, after all, neither mad nor crippled, and I felt only a very clear-minded sadness over my having lost the hope of gambling and the ability to be my own creation.

When we reached the boat, I told my companions to return to Hong Kong without me. I was in control of myself, and there was no reason for us to be together any longer.

"But why?" Peter asked, without any real surprise in his voice.

"I want to see a bit of Macao."

"But you have no guide."

"I don't need one now, Peter."

He started to say something, but then stopped and just smiled. He took my hand and muttered overwrought phrases of gratitude, but in his eyes I clearly saw a look that dismissed me from the circle of the elect, a circle which obviously now included him. The good wishes I'd had for this new gambler began to fade, and I wanted to tell him that if he tried his luck again, he would discover how far from grace he really was.

However, I only told him to buy a decent suit. I then allowed Li Ming and Mei Su to kiss me like nieces and to make promises of fresh delights when I returned to Hong Kong, promises that we all knew would not be kept. As they got into the boat, Li Ming smiled in a way that suggested a secret shared between us, and Mei Su began to string together a melody of obscene farewells. Then, joined by Peter, they waved goodbye and a dismissal as the boat pulled away.

I turned from the harbor, and made my way along the first of several paths that led up the side of a small hill. I was not so fully recovered as I thought, and the climb strained my legs and lungs. But I wanted to reach some vantage point, to see where I was in the world. I had to think, about what had happened and what I must do. Halfway around the world were a few familiar rooms that I could go back to. There I would find unfinished work, letters, love, and all the other projects suitable to a modest talent for living. In those rooms, fear and failure would find sympathy, even encouragement. Safe, ironic and bitter, I could enjoy there a fashionable doom.

When I reached the hilltop, I found myself in front of the uncompleted church I had seen earlier during the ride into town. The pilasters were chipped and split apart; over the vacant portals, headless saints or angels lifted their arms toward heaven while their bodies disappeared in flows of weather-worn drapery; the niches meant for benefactors, apostles or founding fathers were empty. Which had run out first, I wondered, faith or money? Or perhaps faith had been satisfied with a single wall, with keeping up an appearance of devotion.

Suddenly I felt very dizzy and chilled. A light convulsion shook me. I gripped one side of the portal, leaned toward the field it led to so I wouldn't stain the building's wall, and brought up a lumpy gray liquid. Then as I slid slowly down the church wall to the ground, I noticed him. He was dressed like a tourist in a denim suit, open sport shirt, and soft, flopping sunhat. His face was fuller than I would have imagined, but it had the expected sardonic smile, which softened a little the cold weariness in his eyes. He let himself be looked at with patience and did not speak until I turned my gaze from him to the little pool I'd spewed next to me on the ground.

"*Et diabolus vomitor*," he said. "Wouldst send the puky flux for holy inquisition, or thyself search among the gobbets for formucules and menim beldams? Excuse the quaint diction. Just a way of recalling better times, when language was filled with honest words for my meddling. Greet Satan not with clever words but with the wind from an upturned arse. Sound seicento advice, and an appraisal of my powers that flatters me. Of course, nowadays, one puts things differently.

"You shouldn't look surprised. You wanted a meeting with me, and how could I resist such a request, made as it was while stretched out between two whores? Besides, we're both far from our common home, in a godforsaken part of the world. There should be courtesy between us.

"Ah, you think I'm just a symptom of a worn-out mind? Another ugly vision like those you suffered on that floating playhouse? Of course, you've a right to wonder why I'm standing in the shadow of this baroque ruin and talking to a would-be gambler who, if he were to make a Faustian journey, would most likely never survive Auerbach's cellar. I don't mean to be insulting. These are difficult times and the infinite and absolute belong now to mathematics, not to the likes of you and me.

"You flinch at this? You want infernal pacts and pleasures, a hell incurred and a heaven lost? If things were only still so simple, bliss and punishment so precise. Then I might have my horns and pedal deformity, you your dice and cards, and good wagers could be made between us. But now

251

there's nothing to gamble for, nothing of consequence I could win, and nothing of high value you could lose. To pretend otherwise is to play a low trick on one's self, as you have now found out in your rummage through gambling halls and memories. You object to this? Sitting on the edge of China next to your own vomit, you still think there might be some hidden purpose in all the bets you make and the memories that come to mind when you make them. Only the most self-absorbed aesthete believes such things now, someone who dies muttering *qualis artifex pereo,* a public nuisance, a clown of history.

"The excitation, the energy, the joy, despair, manias and mopings—in short the high fevering of life that gambling gave you may once have been the devil's element, but I assure you it is no longer. I've no desire now to take the measure of those whose souls would add heat to hell itself, because I discovered long ago that it's all one whether I trip a Caesar or a fool. All those great battles of will may seem dramatic to you, but they merely wore me out to no purpose. And the world's patience wore out also. Now, you see, I lead a quiet existence, suffered to remain in the world as long as I don't cause great scandals or stay too long in one place. But you want to stir up old desires and bad habits. You want us to gamble, to play for stakes neither of us can afford. You're so desperate to believe in something, you would even believe in me. But I don't want such belief—I'm content to be a rather abstract collection of negative attributes and no longer any man's mortal enemy. So now you see why I had to be harsh with you today, to stultify you for your own good. I had to make it clear that you were wasting my time and yours. And if gambling brings no rewards from me, what can you hope from my opposite?

"No, there is no one to accept the wagers you want to

make. You're bringing no conclusion to your life, you're just making it uncomfortable. Withdraw from the table, my friend. Learn to enjoy the imprecision of things that have no number or color to them. Learn to dream and love in universals. Acquire a taste for paradox and resignation. Diffuse yourself through the world, slip quietly into the calm of pure being, and let us all have a little peace.

"Does the devil sound like a Zen Buddhist? What of it? There is much to be said for the Oriental way of softening life. It is time you abandoned the sharp edges and angles of your precious Gothic spirit. For if you don't, if you force me against will and reason to wrestle you at full strength, then shall you know that the agonies you suffered today were as light caresses when held against my true powers. Oh, I'll hector thee, gambler, gall and pinch thy limbs and wit, compass thee with visions of dark nullity. Thou shalt have no triumph but that some bogle of mine shall whisper it false; no loss, but that it shall seem to thee a kingdom and your soul. Hear me, gambler, if thou wilt be at short swords with the devil, thou shalt be left with a cold purse and bleeding bowels.

"But how I do talk, and again in such a fashion. It's getting time I rejoined my tour. There are some strange things to be seen in Macao. Do you know they have bullfights here? Portuguese bullfights, of course, so there is no killing, no mortal finale. And that is just as well."

He turned and, outlined against the sky's declining light, began walking across the open field. He did not disappear quickly, and I watched him go until, bit by bit, the soft angle of the hill's descent blocked him from view.

And so I had had my visitation, and it had turned out to be no more than a tired scene of genteel *Untergang*. The choice was either to despise or dissolve my life. The only

253

real question was whether I dissolved or despised in comfort, whether, as a wry belletrist or cosmic particle, I had an income sufficient for my needs.

I walked back into Macao filled with practical plans. I thought of the jade and antique shops of Hong Kong, of the things I would buy in them to ornament my rooms in New York. I would also visit the money exchange, and there discover which currencies I should convert my wealth into in order that I might begin to learn the ways of making sure profits. And as I walked and thought of these things, I tried to convince myself that, this time, my journey had not been a failure. I had, after all, learned that life is serious and dangerous, and I'd had the grace, or luck, to realize this while I was still ahead. For, after all, what did all my high notions of gambling come to except a positive addition of money that can be used to make time pass quickly and to buy decent settings for one's metaphysical moments. When I returned home this time it would be with new clothes and exotic presents. I would in every way appear to be a gambler who has won.

While waiting for the ferry back to Hong Kong, I sat in a dockside restaurant and soothed my stomach with warm cups of tea. When the waiter brought the bill, I found, as I went to pay him, that I still had several five- and ten-dollar chips in my pocket, the odd change left over from the purchase at the casino. Smiling, the waiter plucked one from my hand to cover the check and went off staring at it as if he thought he held a truly wonderful object. And, indeed, as I spread the other chips out on the table in front of me, I, too, felt for a moment that they were radiant things. Gold, green, orange, they encased, like pearls or amber, misty undulations of color beneath their surface, gay fusions of light and shadow that made one's thoughts reckless and playful. However, I was not beguiled. I stared critically at the chips until I saw them as nothing more than gaudy medals, tokens of fugitive pleasure. I stacked them neatly on the table and left them as a waiter's tip.

It was midnight when the boat left for Hong Kong. It was a triple-decked ferry, and it moved slowly and quietly through the water. As it drifted along the shoreline lights of Macao, the casino, for a moment, became visible. Lanterns were draped around it like strands of beads, and the dragons, caught in the beams of searchlights, fogged the air with belches of colored smoke. A loudspeaker broadcast the amplified sounds of the casino inside, and thus across the water drifted the murmurs of the shipload of gamblers. I watched and listened until there was only quiet darkness spread out in front of me. I told myself again that I was taking the right route, heading in the direction proper to me.

Later, only for the briefest moment, the dark water beneath me seemed a more honest end. But that was, of course, due only to weariness. Soon the sea air stirred up vigorous thoughts of the people and pleasures that would help me pass the time when I returned. Yes, I would keep a busy schedule, for if the soul finds no true action for itself, it must make do with agitation.

Something like this I told myself as I began the journey home.

ABOUT THE AUTHOR

Jack Richardson was born and educated in New York City. In 1960, with the production of his first play, *Prodigal*, he was hailed as one of the outstanding new playwrights of his generation. After his next three plays were produced, Mr. Richardson left the theater. He has been the recipient of a Guggenheim Fellowship, and his reviews and articles have appeared in *Esquire*, *Commentary*, *Playboy*, *Harper's*, the *New Republic*, and the *New York Review of Books*.